SURRENDER

One Life Divinely Rescued & Lovingly Transformed from Stripper to Saint

DANA McCARTNEY CANDILLO, BSN, RN

A MEMOIR

FORWARD BY LEANNE MATTHESIUS, LEAD PASTOR
C3 CHURCH SAN DIEGO

"I know that this book will bring hope and help to those looking for a way out of the darkness"! – **JACK ELLEDGE, UK DIRECTOR JOYCE MEYER MINISTRIES**

Published by Purpose Publishing
1503 Main Street #168 ♪ Grandview, Missouri
www.purposepublishing.com

ISBN: 978-0-9903010-4-2

Cover design by: Thaddeus Jordan
Cover Photos by: Karen Hacker, The Portrait Gallery
Editing by: Rae Lewis

Printed in the United States of America

This book is available at quantity discounts for bulk purchases. Inquiries may be addressed to the publisher.

www.DanaCandillo.com

Scripture used in this book are noted
from the KJV, NKJV, NLT, HCSB, and AMP versions of the Bible

Praise for Surrendered Showgirl

In Surrendered Showgirl....from Stripper to Saint, I felt the heartbreak of a little girl who just wanted to be unconditionally loved. Dana uses the deep hurts from her past to tell the story of restoration through a redeeming God. This book will touch your heart and remind you that you can never go so far that God's love can't find you.

Annette Westlake
First Lady, Sheffield Family Life Center Kansas City, MO

I met Dana and her LBQ Team at a Christian women's conference and it was an absolute God union. I'm a retired law enforcement officer with 28 years of service. I've had the honor of providing security for Dana and the LBQ Team. I love Dana's heart for women, her boldness and passion to see them live out their God-defined destinies. She is a true survivor and has turned her tragedies into a marvelous testimony. She is caring, generous, wise and just lovely to be around. Her passion to help women is contagious and she is my inspiration! I now serve at the LA Dream Center's Project Hope which helps women in human trafficking and sex slave industries. Dana has taught me so much and has been a wonderful support for me during this challenging endeavor. I know her book will help many people, both women and men, and empower them to be set free and to learn their true identities as precious children of God.

Denise Dailey, Retired Detective
San Diego Police Department

I remember our many talks over lunch concerning your "coming out" with the truth of where you have been and better yet where God has brought you from. You have a testimony, a call, a divine appointment to carry the good news of the Gospel into spiritually dark places. The message you share could not be more timely as we see our culture shifting into an idea that beautiful young ladies (and young men) are mere commodities that can be bought, sold, used and discarded. Thank you for having the courage to trust God with the story He was writing all along. I pray this book will fall into the hands of the many broken young people and through your story they will find hope in the miraculous saving power of Jesus Christ.

With much love, Kathy Taylor, Lead Pastors Wife
Gospel Center Ministries Kansas City, MO

There is nothing more powerful than a testimony of redemption and transformation. Dana has allowed God to restore beauty from ashes as she bravely opens up her life to each of us and shows a beautiful example of pure vulnerably, strength and being an overcomer. You will not be the same after you read this.

Polly Wright , Founder/Executive Director of We Are Cherished
Author of Cherished: Shattered Innocence. Restored Hope.

I *strongly recommend, Surrendered Showgirl....from Stripper to Saint," by Dana McCartney Candillo. It is an absorbing journey that will have you crying and rejoicing as you read about Dana's life from a drug/alcohol surrounded childhood with abuse, through the difficult years of teen, young adulthood with alcohol and dancing in strip clubs, to becoming a new person in Jesus Christ, and being given a great commission by God.*

It is a powerful story of God's redeeming grace; and a testimony to the truth that God loves each of us as if we were the only one He had to love, and we are never gone too far to reach out to Him, because He is always reaching out to us.. It is a book that will give hope to the hopeless, and encourage Christians to step out in faith and be involved in reaching out to hurting people.

Dr. George W. Westlake, Jr., Ph.D. Pastor Emeritus
Sheffield Family Life Center Kansas City, Mo.

Dana McCartney Candillo *is the real deal! She sought our ministry out all the way in Fort Myers and flew in to spend time with us in classes and time with our girls, she really interacted and spoke into their lives. The moment she left they missed her. They had opened up to her that easily. Dana is an amazing woman of God reaching out to those stuck in a life that will destroy them if they don't find their way out! She will help them find their way out!*

Jeanie Turner, Director
One Way Out and His name is Jesus!

Hearing and reading Dana's story is unfortunately a common thread I have heard, seen and dealt with throughout my 24 years on the Kansas City MO Police Department. Ladies that never see their beauty and potential due to years of abuse, alcohol/drugs, and dysfunction in the so called "home". Reaching for the only way out, they are easily trafficked by those who appear to be friends only to find out it's just another lie of Satan. This book is about **REALITY** *right in our community! I applaud Dana for being transparent, telling her story, standing up as a model of hope for those victimized and being an example to the Christian community to show the love of Jesus. What a testimony of transformation.*

Cindy Cotterman, Sergeant
Kansas City, MO Police Department

Dana's memoir is a remarkable story about an extraordinary woman who "against all odds" in the world's economy emerged from one of the darkest places on earth; a woman redeemed and restored by the grace and mercy of Jesus Christ! Her story will break your heart as you travel the journey of her early life and leave you rejoicing as you experience her true redemption and ultimate restoration...

Roger & Lynne Horne, Lead Pastors
Lee's Summit First Church, Lee's Summit, MO

"Dana's story is an amazing testimony of how God's grace can dramatically change any life no matter what the circumstance! As her past comes to life on the pages of her book you will discover the brutal reality of abuse, abandonment, and pain that unquestionably marks her childhood and young adult years. Yet in spite of all this, she did not let it define her or rob her of the beautiful life God had planned for her. You will see how God saved Dana from a life of destruction and bondage and brought her into a place of strength and dignity which later positioned her to bring healing, restoration and the message of salvation to other women who are still lost, hurting and hopeless. I believe this book will be a rewarding experience for all who read it, and should challenge us all to be willing to let God use our own personal, unedited, and authentic story as a way of reaching out to others who may find strength in seeing how the love of Christ can change lives!"

Pastor Lisa Purkey
Nexus Church Olathe, KS

God's everlasting beauty is evident in the healing and transformational work of the Holy Spirit. Dana's life journey, is packed with the evidence of His Living Power that is readily available to all who desire to receive it. With many tears, I read the real life struggles of a precious young girl and rejoiced as she decided to pursue life to the fullest with all God's intentions. God pursued her, loved her and restored her. True joy is found as God expands His territories and His borders. As God continues to do this for Dana, this book will be an encouragement to you, as you continue to pursue God's fullness within life's journey.

Dr. Fel & Mrs. Dianna Bagunu
GracePointe Community Church Lee's Summit, MO

In Surrendered Showgirl....from Stripper to Saint, Dana Candillo, bares her soul and honestly shares her personal struggles in answering God's calling on her life into ministry. Her transformation has brought insight to this very controversial subject. Dana Candillo helps women throw off the shackles of bondage and break the chains of sexual exploitation so they can walk in the freedom that God has destined for their life. This book will inspire you to reach those who are searching for the Father's Love!

Pastor Willie and Dr. Vickie Murillo
Sheffield Family Life Center, Kansas City, MO

Surrendered Showgirl is such a marvelous revelation of how God can take what seems to be overwhelming circumstances in a person's life and make something beautiful and highly valued out of it. In this book Dana McCartney Candillo has shown us the dark and ugly side of the world and at the same time the light and freedom that God can bring. I know that this book will bring hope and help to those looking for a way out of the darkness.

Jack Elledge, UK Director
Joyce Meyer Ministries

I believed that my appearance and my body was my only resource. I began relying on them after the early child sexual abuse started. I began wearing heavy makeup, tight clothes, and a bleeding heart. I was on the search for "real love". My mother was a severe alcoholic and drug addict and my father was in prison. Choices were few; structure, guidance and love were exempt. Survival was in full force.

I was full of unmet needs, desires, and wants. I had no goals, dreams, or ambition. Wading through the emotions of the tragic loss of my early childhood, my grandmother; "mom" was the only parent I once had. With her passing at my young age of 7, I was on an emotional roller coaster with no one to turn to. I was lost and trying to survive in a world of dysfunction, poverty, addictions and poor decisions of adults as well as my own.

In this memoir, From Stripper to Saint, I tell my life story. From an early childhood of many forms of abuse, neglect and uncertainty, to a teenage rebellion, completely out of control. I was on a desperate search for love and affection always to find a dead-end. My first marriage was to a male stripper who landed in prison and second marriage, a wealthy businessman in which material things couldn't bring happiness. Inside the strip club I thought I found attention, financial means, affection and security. I thought I found myself. Truly I lost myself. I became someone else. Twenty years ago in January of 1994 when I least expected it...the Power of God invaded my heart and life and brought the Transforming Truth to my life. I was literally gripped and pulled out of my personal Hell.

In telling my story I hope to inspire and encourage women that there is hope and light at the end of the tunnel. There is no distance too far for God to Reach. His love is limitless and unconditional."

A Personal Word from the Author

Before you begin to read and process this story, I want you to know that I am so very delighted and excited for you to experience the Glory in the End. However, the end would make no sense if the beginning were not told. We cannot dwell, live in, or continue looking back as to what is left behind. We MUST push forward toward the future and live in the NOW! "I press on to reach the end of the race and receive the heavenly prize for which God, through Christ Jesus, is calling us." Philippians 3:14 NLT

This story was written with absolutely no intent of harming anyone and is purposed with the clear intent of guiding others struggling with similar backgrounds, bondages, addictions, and struggles with direction toward FREEDOM through Jesus Christ, Our Lord and Savior!

I desperately pray that you know that it is of extreme importance to me that the persons and life experiences captured throughout the story should NOT be judged or dishonored regarding the circumstances. The past is just that: The Past! The people portrayed throughout my journey all remain close to me and my only sole intent in sharing specific details is to reflect on the end result which is the marvelous Glory of our God! "Do not judge others, and you will not be judged." Matthew 7:1 NLT and "He who is without sin among you, let him throw a stone at her first." John 8:7b NKJV

Truly this story contains two radical life transforming testimonies. One is mine and the other is my mother's. Decades have passed, much grace, healing, restoration, change, and 100% FORGIVENESS has transpired. So I ask you in advance to please hold on to nothing negative, as I am completely FREE, so is she, and so should you be! For Surely HE IS GOOD and MERCIFUL!

Though my personal journey was a season of great difficulty; through this story I choose to publically forgive. As well, I give credit to my mother for inviting me to church, into a new environment filled with His presence, where I made the greatest decision of my life. My decision and commitment to Christ has led me to my destiny. Today, I am fully aware of my true born identity and my eternity. In forgiveness peace abides. I trust this story will help others walk in forgiveness and freedom; be made whole.

Graced in Oceans Deep,

Dana

I am a personal friend of Dana's mom and can testify how God has changed her and worked miracles in her life. She is a dear friend and fellow sister in Christ. She is a true testament of how God sees all of us as being witnesses for His Kingdom.

Long time Family friend,

'Shared stories build a relational bridge that Jesus can walk across from your heart to others'.

Rick Warren, The Purpose Drive Life ©

A Personal Word from Dana's Husband
Rocky Candillo

Wow, was my first impression! As I'm sitting in church and see a beautiful blonde. I think to myself; who is that gorgeous lady? Upon leaving the service, I am introduced to her by a mutual friend. As I was leaving, I turn around to glance at her again and she's looking back at me. This was the beginning of this crazy little thing called love for Dana and I! As we got to know each other, she began to share her past with me. Dana opened up about the pains and pitfalls, the tragedies and triumphs in her life and said to me, "I may not be the girl for you". I knew she was now born again and I could not hold her past against her. In fact, if many of us were to share things from our past we could all bury our heads in shame and embarrassment. So, who am I to hold Dana's past against her or anyone else for that matter? People may question how I'm okay with my wife revealing her past lifestyle. You might ask if it bothers me? It would bother me more to stand in judgment. *II Corinthians 5:17 (NLT) This means anyone who belongs to Christ has became a new person the old life is gone a new life has begun!* I have had a front row seat and witnessed the full metamorphosis of what has taken place in Dana's life Overcoming the fear and anxiety that used to rule her life has now given way to peace, hope and faith.

Dana is bold in her passion to share the love of God with hurting people wherever they may be. It doesn't matter if it's in the store, in the hair salon or in a strip club. She wants everyone to know what Jesus has done in this *Surrendered Showgirls* life!

I am very proud of Dana. The way she has allowed the power of God to use her is as beautiful as she is; inside and out. Her story is a Paradox! It shows us that by surrendering our life to GOD; we gain it back! John 10:10 (MSG) states, *I came so they can have real and eternal life, more and better life than they ever dreamed of.* I am a very proud husband!

Te Amo
Tu Esposo
Rocky

The Bridge

For years, I would enter into my house late at night after work, many times drunk and in a wasted state of mind. I would find myself staring at one of my favorite pictures hanging on the wall of my living room. It was a popular home interior picture, at that time, of a beautiful brook with flowers surrounding it and an arched grey stone bridge painted over the rippled spring. This picture was a representation of my life and I named it, "A Bridge Over Troubled Water". I thought my life was like 'the bridge' just holding up over the mess of all my problems and circumstances. My thoughts would make me believe I was strong like the stone bridge; I could survive and stay braced for anything.

Thinking back now, it's possible that God allowed me to visualize that picture in that way. He had an extraordinary plan that one day He would allow me to recognize as he revealed it. A mighty plan to be a bridge over and across a great divide. A bridge that troubled water could become calm and flow into a river of peace. A bridge set apart with a *divine destiny* and *purpose*. In the Book, *"The Purpose Driven Life"*, Rick Warren states it best when he says, 'Shared stories build a relational bridge that Jesus can walk across from your heart to others'. Perhaps the picture on the living room wall was one of prophetic purpose and promise for me. Today, I say "Yes" to my story being that bridge. I pray that those who make the decision to cross it, holding the hand of Jesus, will never look back to what they left on the other side!

Dana

WARNING: Subject matter and descriptive content in this book may not be suitable for readers under eighteen years of age.

NOTE: While this story is of true account, some of the names have been changed to protect the privacy of the persons involved.

SPECIAL NOTE: This book contains my perspective and opinions that may not be considered actual facts in the minds of those persons cited.

The Biblical Definition of "SAINTS"

And He personally gave some to be apostles, some prophets, some evangelists, some pastors and teachers, [12] for the training of the SAINTS in the work of ministry, to build up the body of Christ, [13] until we all reach unity in the faith and in the knowledge of God's Son, growing into a mature man with a stature measured by Christ's fullness. [14] Then we will no longer be little children, tossed by the waves and blown around by every wind of teaching, by human cunning with cleverness in the techniques of deceit. [15] But speaking the truth in love, let us grow in every way into Him who is the head—Christ. [16] From Him the whole body, fitted and knit together by every supporting ligament, promotes the growth of the body for building up itself in love by the proper working of each individual part. Ephesians 4:11-16, HCSB

To the church of God which is at Corinth, to those who are sanctified in Christ Jesus, called to be SAINTS, with all who I every place call on the name of Jesus Christ our Lord, both theirs and ours. I Corinthians 1:2, NKJV

But the SAINTS of the Most High shall receive the kingdom, and possess the kingdom forever and ever. Daniel 7:18, NKJV

"I Surrender" by Hillsong

Here I am
Down on my knees again
Surrendering all
Surrendering all

Find me here
Lord as You draw me near
Desperate for You
Desperate for You

I surrender

Drench my soul
As mercy and grace unfold
I hunger and thirst
I hunger and thirst

With arms stretched wide
I know You hear my cry
Speak to me now
Speak to me now

I surrender
I surrender
I wanna know You more
I wanna know You more

Like a rushing wind
Jesus breathe within
Lord have Your way
Lord have Your way in me

A Special Dedication

"To My Daughters"

May you direct your lives in the ways of the Lord forever and be surrounded by his amazing love, protection, provision and favor all the days of your lives!

"A Special Dedication To My Sister"

I was recently made aware that my sister spent the last days of her young life on the streets of Kansas City due to her childhood background, incarceration and destructive path.

I pray that through this book, I can somehow bring honor to her life and make a difference in women's lives in the Kansas City area and around the world!!

"It was the first time I entered a strip club, I remember walking under a dark bridge, shuffling through the gravel. The door flung open and up the old rickety stairs I went. It was dirty and nothing what I expected...but money was flying everywhere. Within moments of being in the strip club my bills were no longer my problem, my soul became my problem.

Dedications

"To the Brokenhearted..."

"I tell you, her sins – and they are many – have been forgiven, so she has shown me much love. But a person who is forgiven little shows only little love." Luke 7:47 NLT

This book is for ALL Women....and dedicated to those who have been abused, neglected, suffered child-abuse, molestation, suffered poverty, gone hungry, have been a single parent, cheated on, abandoned, hurt, betrayed, threatened, physically or sexually abused, assaulted, battered, been fatherless, left alone, motherless, lied to, deceived, divorced, re-married, in a blended family, struggled with sexual promiscuity, grown up under alcoholism and drug abuse, chosen alcohol and drugs, exploited themselves for money, done things with regrets, been sex trafficked, experienced being a stripper, been married to or dated a stripper....been a spouse of an inmate, tried to get out from under a desperate situation, been dominated, had abortions, had miscarriages and infertility issues, struggled with anxiety, depression, hopelessness and powerlessness, been on welfare housing, struggled with a low-end job to try to make it, experienced the death of a parent as a child, has had a parent in the prison system, born to a teenage mother, raised by grandparents, lived under social judgment, fears and insecurities, been broke and nowhere to go...and last but not least, have a willingness and a teachable spirit with a desire to CHANGE &/OR OVERCOME?!

This book is also for ALL women who have experienced birthing healthy children, a Christian relationship in marriage, been church go-ers, benchwarmers, evangelists, pastor's wives, board member's wives, in the church choir, lived in a Christian bubble – full of fear of judg-ment/condemnation, been born again and set free, saved, filled with the Holy Spirit, a worshipper, worked in a ministry of controversial subjects, experienced judgment in church, experienced acceptance as well as grace and mercy, experienced love and respect, experienced success, made wealthy and blessed financially, have lived blessed lives with all outer needs met, wanted for nothing, living in no lack, experi-enced hurt/pain inside the church, or experienced abuse of power in the church. Additionally, if you had favor poured out on your life, been educated, earned degrees, held professional licenses, been given limitless opportunities and are living for God and striving for Heaven, this book is for you, too!

I've experienced ALL of the above in my life and I am finally content with the girl in the beginning of my life journey and the woman that I am today. I've analyzed and learned much about people, the world and most of all, GOD! God can take your mess and make it your message. As you read this book, please be open-minded and prayerful that HE can and will heal your wounded heart and use you for His Glory if you will allow Him to. He is all knowing, all powerful and forgiving…. He is a great God – His name is Jesus Christ. I pray by the end of this book, you will make a life decision to receive Him, fol-low Him and experience a gracious and extraordinary life, a life trans-formed by the power of Jesus Christ!

All For Him,

Dana McCartney Candillo

Table of Contents

Money rushed through my hands like water yet had a high price tag and consequences attached to it. The lights flashed, the stage was set and the mask was on. It was glitz and glamour for 7 ½ years, a facade of lies. I felt alone, an outcast of society, and in my own world of false power and illusion of wealth. I was entrapped in total darkness.

Acknowledgements

For many years, writing this book has been on my mind. I felt the Lord speak to me in 1994 shortly after I had given my life to him. I knew the name of it then as well. What I did not know was if I really could handle putting myself "out there". What I was sure of was that he would never leave me nor forsake me! (So be strong and courageous! Do not be afraid and do not panic before them. For the Lord your God will personally go ahead of you. He will neither fail you nor abandon you. Deuteronomy 31:16, NLT) I am so thankful for the Mercy and Grace of Jesus! With that I become "free", more and more each day! We cannot choose our parents, our childhood environment, economic status, or most decisions that adults make for us as children. I can say that although I would've never chosen the childhood that was dealt to me, I can choose to honor and respect both of my parents whether they deserve it or not, in the best way that I know how. I thank them and release them both. I thank them, that through them, I have this life, and I release them from the pains and hardships of the past. I thank my husband, Rocky Candillo for not being judgmental of me from day one! Thank you for believing in me and supporting me, thank you for your un-denying commitment and faithfulness to God. Special thanks to my beautiful daughters Alayna, Lauren, and Marissa, and daughter-in-law Jessica who are lovely and priceless to me and for their support and encouragement to help other girls and women make a difference. I thank my son Michael and son-in-law Mario for support and encouragement and most of all for leading and guiding our grandchildren, Colton, Cruz, Aydin and Ava in the direction of the Lord, Jesus Christ! (Train up a child in the way he should go, and when he is old he will not depart from it. Proverbs 22:6, NLT) I am ever so thankful for an awesome Board of Directors and spouses who stepped up and backed us with incredible support, which boosted my confidence and aided me to move forward. Thank you Dr. Fel & Dianna Bagunu, Pastor Roger & Lynne Horne, and Pastor Willie & Dr. Vickie Murillo.

My most extraordinary gratitude to Dr. George Westlake, Jr. whom I have no idea where I would be today but for his faithfulness to the call of the ministry and allowing Jesus to move through him. There truly are NO WORDS to explain the influence and difference his ministry has made in my life! It was under his ministry that I was gripped and released from the fiery pit of my life to my process of a radical transformation, One Life Transformed by the Power of Jesus Christ!

A very special thanks to Pastor Jon & Lisa Purkey of Nexus Church, Olathe, Kansas; who upon first meeting me, believed in me, the ministry, and swiftly stepped in to help me in many ways including financial support!

A very personal thanks to the entire Westlake Family for their unwavering commitment to "The Call" and limitless efforts to raise up the Sheffield Family Life Center to be an all-encompassing and welcoming place of acceptance and love, a church where every person walking through their doors may surely feel comfortable. A special thank you and appreciation to Heather Veitch, Founder of JC's Girls who braved the path before me with great courage and blazed the trail for ministry to the sex industry. Her example moved me, inspired me, and touched my life. Thank you to ALL my LBQ girls and co-laborers in this unique and remarkable ministry, Elena, Starla, Rachel, and ALL the dear and special ladies who help with so many things; packaging gifts, prayer, security, and giving of their time, talents and energy!! I could not do what I am doing with excellence if it were not for each and every person doing their part! How Blessed I am!! A special thank you to Lynne Horne, First Lady at Lee's Summit Assembly who has listened tirelessly to me and helped me with so many LBQ projects! A very special thank you to Linda Westlake Francisco who has poured her heart, time, and determination into grant writing for LBQ with such diligence and creativity in hopes that we may continue and grow and expand a successful and fruitful ministry! Thank you to Pastor Fel & Dianna Bagunu at Grace Pointe Community, who first believed in me and have given and supported the ministry financially from the beginning!

Thank you to Pastor George Westlake III for giving of yourself in time and counseling with me prior to stepping out on this journey.

Your insight and years of ministry helped guide me as I sought direction and planning. "Our vision for lost souls and for Kansas City is like-minded!" To Annette Westlake, First Lady of Sheffield Family Life Center, you are the sweetest, most honest, trustworthy and Godliest woman I know! Thank you for years of friendship and your support! To Tom and Stephanie Moore, Wow! No words can say how much favor from you both has blessed our personal lives and ministry! God surely used you both in many ways as instruments to this ministry. Tom, if I had not known you, LBQ would not exist today as it is! Last but not least, a most grateful appreciation to Lisa Bevere and Messenger International! In a miraculous and divine way, God boldly used Lisa Bevere's bestselling book "Lioness Arising" to speak prophetically into my life and move me from my comfort zone into the realm of my calling!! Thank you to all who have sown into this ministry and covered it in prayer from the beginning. Thank you Kathy McCartney Taylor, my aunt, who I very first took LBQ to, as just an "idea"! I love you All! With a grateful and sincere heart,

P.S. To Many of my favorite ministers who have answered the call to ministry via television ministry – Your love for Jesus and desire to reach the nations has blessed and taught me – you each reached my household!!

℘ Joyce Meyer	℘ Joni & Marcus Lamb	℘ Mike Murdock
℘ T.D. Jakes	℘ Beth Moore	℘ The Crouch Family
℘ Joel Osteen	℘ James & Betty Robison	℘ Jentezen Franklin

Foreword

"If story's of Gods rescue, redemption and restoration move and encourage you then Dana Candillo's book is for you. Dana's moving and at times shocking life story, shows us how God wants to rescue and reach us even in our deepest pit and darkest despair. Throughout the Bible, God's signature is seen through stories of triumph in the midst of tragedy, light in the midst of great darkness and hope and courage when things seem utterly hopeless. Dana shows us through her story that God is not afraid of getting involved in our messes and just like His word says, He is a very present help in our time of trouble! Her testimony of God's power to transform, His enduring faithfulness and relentless pursuit of His children is one that will inspire, encourage and bring hope to so many.

Dana's bravery is inspirational!! Her selfless passion to save people who were caught in the same lie and prison that she herself was once a prisoner of will challenge us all to take up our cross and be carriers of Gods message of grace to a world that so desperately needs to hear it!

Congratulations Dana for having the courage to tell your story it will be the catalyst of freedom for so many!"

Leanne Matthesius. Lead Pastor
C3 Church San Diego, California

Preface

"Surrendered Showgirl.....from Stripper to Saint" reveals the pain, fear, and internal struggles of being in the commercial sex industry from the perspective of a woman who has survived it. Dana describes how for some people, life is a setup, creating the perfect victim. As a survivor of prostitution/sex trafficking, I appreciate how Dana explains the stigma of those involved in "the life" and how some of that remains in your mind and heart years after exiting the life. Dana beautifully proclaims her love for God and rejoices in His love and grace for her. Embracing God's perfect love is essential for hope, healing, and restoration for those escaping the commercial sex industry.

Ignorant & stagnant communities see a stripper and/or a prostitute;
Informed & educated communities see a victim;
Responsive & courageous communities make a difference!

**Kristy Childs - Survivor - Founder, Executive Director
Veronica's Voice, Inc.**

Prologue

"Dearly Beloved, We are gathered here together to get through this thing called Life" by Prince

From the very beginning, in Genesis, God created each and every one of us as His marvelous work and craftsmanship. Each one His Masterpiece. He made each person so unique and detailed. His masterful design was for each spiritual being to embrace the human being experience and have an authentic and personal relationship with Him, our Creator. As this journey begins, it doesn't take long for us to recognize our desperate need for Him. Traveling through winding roads, mountaintops, and hills and valleys we each write our very own unique and personal story. Each of our stories are woven into the intricate fabric of His story.

For so many years I sat in silence, wondering "What if?"

What if I could make a difference?

What if I could play a part in which something could change the direction of another woman or person's story?

What if that lost little girl could dream again and know that it was okay for her to do that?

What if seeds of greatness could be planted that would ultimately take root and burst forth with the knowledge and truth that we are equal and are deserving of Love, Value, Purpose and Dignity?...

A priceless treasure by His design.

I pondered and pondered these thoughts of how I could "go back" and create change in the dark atmosphere of the sex industry. Seldom do little girls say, "When I grow up I want to become a stripper or a prostitute!" So many times "Life" takes us to places we never imagined we would be, doing things we said we would never do, and act in ways we never believed we would behave. Most of the time, the causes that lead up to the pit we fall into are symptoms of unmet needs, abuses, emotional deficiencies and sheer survival. I have found that "ONLY" the "LOVE" of God can cure and fill that empty void in the human heart.

My decision to carry that love ("the Cross") into the darkness and into the world of exotic dancing was ultimately having faith and believing that just as Jesus and the 12 disciples changed the world... So can you and I! ("*Many times our pain is our pulpit!*" ~ T.D. Jakes[1]) His word declares, "Go ye into all the world..." – sharing the Gospel – The Great Commission, Matt. 28:16-20 KJV. Jesus loves ALL people. He did not come for the healthy – He came for the sin sick! He went to Matthew's House! – He is LOVE to ALL People! God is no respecter of persons! He came to fix this broken life... Period.

After nearing 20 years as a new Woman in Christ, (This means that anyone who belongs to Christ has become a new person. The old life

30

is gone, a new life has begun! 2 Corinthians 5:17 NLT) I knew that I could not hold back any longer. I knew that I had found the answer; the harvest is ripe and the workers are few. I knew that I needed to trust Him 100% and step my foot out onto the water. I did have fear. I was concerned. Was I willing to do what I knew He had asked me to do in order to fulfill His plan and His purpose in my life? My reasoning was self-preservation and protection from the thoughts of other people in the church (as well as outside of the church). That is exactly what the enemy wants us to think and cause us to walk right out of our calling!

As night falls we drive for hours on the dark city streets, with bright neon lights and signs flashing we are clearly on a mission; a mission of Love and Hope. Our minds and hearts race with anticipation of all of the awesome God moments and divine appointments that we "know" we are about to encounter. In those moments are genuine and authentic exchanges of unexplainable worth. There are times that I've felt a love, appreciation, and thankfulness far greater than I have ever felt in church or in "Christian circles." I pray that this ministry breaks down barriers and attitudes of religiosity and judgmental spirits and is a true example of "carrying our cross".

God's Love is so powerful and explosive! It can move and do unimaginable things in any environment, circumstance, and life! It moves in ways that feel electric, like wind, like water, like rain and like the air that we breathe. When it is carried into the places as directed, it will do ALL that is needed to do! It flows like a rushing river covering every heart of stone. As we walk through the club doors time after time I am confident that His presence is with me and where He goes I will follow.

This is My Story…A Love Story for the King.

The First Trimester

"Double for your former trouble..."
"Instead of your shame, you shall have double honor, and instead of confusion, they shall rejoice in their own portion. Therefore, in their own land, they shall possess double; everlasting joy will be theirs." ~Isaiah 61:7 NKJV

"Return to the stronghold, you prisoners of hope. Even today I declare that I will restore double to you." ~Zechariah 9:12 NKJV

"And the LORD restored Job's losses when he prayed for his friends. Indeed the LORD gave Job twice as much as he had before." ~Job 42:10 NKJV

"The Story of Beauty" by *Destiny's Child*

Please dry your eyes young girl, don't cry, you're beautiful
It's not your fault, young girl, don't cry, you're beautiful
You're not the one to blame
Soon it will be okay, one day you'll realize your beauty

He touched her places that he shouldn't have touched
He did some things to her that he shouldn't have done

She looked for her father in the men that she saw in,
Thought that all she had to offer was her body,
No one could figure out why this young girl would live her life,
In such pain and unhappiness because she was so beautiful
She rebelled and one day the young girl fell in love with another
man like her dad
He abused her emotionally and made her feel like she was
worthless
I hope one day she realizes, and sees the beauty in her eyes,
All she needs is prayer and strength because she's beautiful

"Not Afraid" by *Eminem*

I am not afraid, I am not afraid
To take a stand, to take a stand
Yeah it's been a ride
Everybody, everybody
I guess I had to
Come take my hand, come take my hand
Go to that place and get to this one

We'll walk this world together through the storm
Now some of you
Whatever weather, cold or warm
Might still be in that place
Just lettin' you know that you're not alone
If you're tryin' to get out
Holla if you feel like you've been down the same road
Just follow me, I'll get you there

Chapter 1 - Victim
My Childhood

It was the spring of 1977 and my life was about to change drastically. I was seven years old, tiny and beautiful – with my hair in perfect brunette curls and a white ribbon. My dress, powder-blue short-sleeved chiffon, tailor made for a doll and white patent leather shoes. On the outside, I was a pretty little princess, quiet and still. As I passed by "Mom's" casket, I was filled with emotion and confusion… would she ever wake up? On the inside, scared and scattered, wondering where I should be, who's going to take care of me? Up until this point, life, although dysfunctional, seemed somewhat safe and secure. But the cold hard truth was that "mom" was really my step-grandmother raising me, with my alcoholic grandfather, by herself. Born a fatherless child to their seventeen year old daughter, my biological mother was addicted to drugs and alcohol, lived "upstairs" and was not permitted to parent me. She had too many problems of her own, dealing with the guilt and shame and hurt of an unwanted teenage pregnancy in 1969. Becoming pregnant at sixteen years old was frowned upon and treated with rejection. But certainly and surely, I was someone's daughter after all…wasn't I?

Many years later I learned the answer to that question was YES! The Daughter of a King – Jesus – who reveals to me:

"For you are my offspring" (Acts 17:28)

"I knew you even before you were born/conceived" (Jeremiah 1:5)

"I chose you when I planned creation." (Ephesians 1:11)

"You were not a mistake, for all your days are written in my Book" (Psalm 139:16)

"I determined the exact time of your birth and where you would live" (Acts 17:26)

"You are fearfully and wonderfully made" (Psalm 139:14)

"I knit you together in your mother's womb" (Psalm 139:13)

"And brought you forth on the day you were born" (Psalm 71:6)

Thank you, Father God that Your hand was upon me from the very beginning! As a very small child, I can recall some peace and normalcy. "Mom" loved me as her own…she was childless. She was always cooking and baking; pies, cookies, cakes, yummy dinners, anything that I asked for. She catered to me. She hand-sewed my clothes on her sewing machine, taught me how to write and paint and play games. She took me to church; just the two of us, on occasion. She shared a bedroom with me; she kept me "SAFE". I would run wildly through the house when my grandpa came home from work, with his metal lunchbox in hand, and our dog, Fritz, leaping and running in circles, and barking. All seemed fairly normal but as night fell, it was another story. Every night my grandpa

She shared a bedroom with me; she kept me "SAFE".

would sit in his chair, in front of the television, and get stone-cold drunk. Empty bottles filled the bottom of his chair and "Mom" cleaned it out daily. I could hear my real mother who lived upstairs playing the guitar, drunk and listening to loud music. I wasn't allowed to go up there except on rare occasions. If and when she ever came to dinner, it was a knock down drag out fight between her and my grandpa. So this rarely happened. There was a constant battle between the two of them. Fights often broke out about who was going to burn the house down first, falling asleep with their cigarette burning, smoking and kill us all. In 1969, when he first found out that his daughter was pregnant, she expressed to me that, he would make her hide in closets when relatives came over, trying to hide her – running from pride and shame, he eventually moved her out of state to remain in secrecy as long as possible. She explained, as she was about to give birth, he brought her home and strangely and quietly explained this to the family and then ignored the situation and resorted to his dark life of alcoholism. She took a night job, made little money, dropped out of high school and gained no further education. Today, she continues to reminisce about the pain of being a 16 year old girl, pregnant, boarding a train and walking in the cold windy streets of Chicago alone waiting for her connection on the train. The enemy seeks to devour, kill and destroy…. (John 10:10) She was filled with bitterness and hatred. The boy who had gotten her pregnant was 18 and married, with a son already and long gone from her life. Later, he headed for prison. Alcohol and drugs soon became the preferred choice of coping mechanisms for my mother.

In the spring of 1977, I was made aware she had a nervous breakdown at the same time that, in a different hospital, "Mom" passed away. At this time I stayed with my Aunt Jan, who lived up the street. She cared for me, wanted to adopt me and quickly became the idol of a seven year old, scared and lonely little girl. She was kind and wealthy and I wanted to be just like her when I grew up. My Aunt Jan had a great and positive influence on my life. Her house was peaceful and seemed calm. It was probably the closest thing to normalcy that I had ever known. There was no drunkenness or drug usage going on there. Her house was <u>very</u> fancy; picture perfect. She was constantly on the move cleaning and cooking and taking meticulous care of her home. Everything sparkled! Everything was always clean and fresh. She kept her house immaculate and beautiful. I thought it would be a dream come true to live in that house, like a fairy tale. I remember dancing and skipping all throughout the rooms and imagining that I lived there. She was always very warm and kind towards me and would say she would take me as her own if she could. She was so beautiful to me, I thought she was glamorous and I wanted to be just like her when I grew up. She would never leave her house without being made up and looking picture perfect. Not even to go to the grocery store! When my "mom" died, I remember her taking me to a week-long Bible school at a church shortly afterward. I remember receiving a tiny necklace there that had a small clear round piece with a grain of a mustard seed inside of it. I thought this was so special. How could that be all the faith that one would need? I was captured by the Bible school teacher's explanation of it! I probably wore that necklace all summer long. I stayed with my aunt a lot; as much as I could. She would take me to school when I stayed the night there and she would always get up extra early to make me chocolate chip pancakes and juice. She had two sons but she never had a daughter of her own. My biological mother was named after her; I called her Janis. I did not understand that she was really my mother. My Aunt Jan broke the news to me, on her knees, that my grandmother, "Mom", had died and Janis was sick and in the hospital so I would be living with her for a little while. I liked that idea but I was also devastated and very sad to have lost my "Mom!" Aunt Jan took me shopping for the blue dress at a special boutique and had my hair done; making sure that I was picture-perfect for the funeral service. I stared, clutching her hand, during the entire service. Walking by the casket as my "Mom's" lifeless body laid there, I knew my life would never be the same. I clung to Aunt Jan and sat next to her in the black, long, scary limousine to the gravesite. After that day, anytime I passed down that street, I could never look in that direction. I begged and cried to stay with my Aunt. I suffered severe separation anxiety from my "Mom" anytime she was away from me and now she was gone forever; the only safe place left for me was with my Aunt Jan, but unfortunately, that just wasn't going to happen. I remember several phone calls sitting at her kitchen table as she battled with Janis on the phone about adopting me. One thing I've learned is that you cannot talk or reason with alcohol or drugs. Years later, as my Aunt grew cold and tired of the situation, realizing that she was paralyzed to really be able to do anything, she cut ties with Janis. That meant the ties and connection was gone from me as well. This was really heartbreaking. I loved her very much. If we saw her in public, she did not even speak to us anymore. Years went by like this. It was horrible rejection. She was the only living blood relative on Janis' maternal side of the family. In recent past years, I had the chance to visit and see her once again. She was in the hospital in terrible condition with terminal cancer. Recently, I was in St. Louis at a Joyce Meyer conference and received a phone call that my dear Aunt Jan had passed away. I was unable to make it back for the funeral. I felt the loss but God must have had a reason for me not being there at that time. Unfortunately, she and my mother were on poor terms and never spoke again at the time of her death – a true regret!

So, eventually, the inevitable happened, I had to return to that big, empty, cold house on Park Street where my "Mom" no longer lived. I was left with Janis and Grandpa; a fine pair of hurt, incapable individuals, bitter and angry and negative toward life; drowning their emptiness in whiskey and beer and drugs and a lifestyle that no child should be allowed to endure. Any prior memory I had of being alone with Janis was abusive. When, on rare occasions, my "Mom" did let her take me somewhere or spend a little time with me, it was filled with lies and abuse. She told me to tell them I fell down when I returned one time with a bruise on my body. She would tell them she wanted to take me bowling, but instead we went to a bar. One horrific night, she told them she was taking me somewhere fun and we did not return until the next day. She was on a date with, what I remember to be a fat, ugly, awful man, named Eugene, in a Volkswagen bug and they kept driving us in circles telling me just to be quiet, that we were going home to "Mom's" house but I knew it was a lie. Instead, we went into a cold, dark, old and empty house with a couch in a room – that was it. I was told to lie down and go to sleep – I was crying; they were drunk and in the bedroom with the door open. I was freezing and could not go to sleep for the horrible sounds and had to go to the bathroom so bad but I was forced to hold it all night. The only way to the bathroom meant I had to pass by them. In the morning I tip-toed past them quietly and frightened to get to the bathroom. They just laid there and I wanted to throw up. I was angry and wanted to go home. I did not trust her or like her and I wanted to go home. I had to lie to my wonderful "Mom" about where we'd been all night.

Now with her gone, my life was headed for complete and utter chaos! How and why would God allow this to happen to an innocent seven year old girl? Every day was a nightmare adventure in my once safe and lovely home on Park Street. I would frequently run away, up the street to my Aunt Jan's and beg her to call the police and keep me forever. Then the banging at the door would start; Janis and Grandpa, both drunk, demanding their child. I quickly began to dislike, even hate, my life. Shortly after I turned 8 years old, my mother met John; a very nice, Italian man, who wanted to marry her, and was kind to me, never lifting a finger physically toward me. Unfortunately, however, he was also a full-blown alcoholic. He had pornographic magazines throughout the house and quickly began filling up the basement with marijuana plants growing them under special lights and tending regularly to his precious garden. They fought constantly, violently, and there was always a party at our house and no food. We were incredibly poor and lived in a trashy, filthy house filled with fleas. But there somehow was always money for alcohol, cigarettes, pornography and drugs. One night, I woke up to a cigarette burning, loud music playing that left my mother lying in the living room floor crying "Help me!" Her head was cracked open with blood running out. I was swiftly and instantly being turned into her caretaker. I found myself pouring peroxide on her wounds and bandaging her head because John threw her causing her head to hit the end table. Somehow I was becoming the parent and she the child. She was a sad case. At times they would fight. I recall an incident when she went outside in a blizzard, barefoot with me chasing her to get her back into the house. It also became a daily occurrence without fail for her to be drunk and driving the car with us in it. She would often misplace her keys; therefore, we were locked out of the house. She would lift me, while laughing, and push me through a tiny window over the kitchen table. Then, I would fall and run to the door, unlock it (so maybe) we could go to bed and sleep.

Somehow I figured out a church bus came by our home on Sunday mornings so I would get up and escape while everyone slept with hangovers. The church bus picked me up and took me clear across town to a Baptist Church. I walked to the eight year old class all by myself and I remember trying to stand up and recite all the books of the Bible in order; Genesis, Exodus, Leviticus, etc. I had no parents there to listen. She did not even know where I was. I was there with all the other eight year olds and felt like I just wasn't normal and did not fit in anywhere. Something was just wrong with me. I felt that way at school too, I did not understand assignments or what I was supposed to be doing. I would get up and go to church many Sundays on that bus and she never knew I was missing – she would say later that she just figured I went to church. She was mean, belligerent, and violent when she was drunk.

One horrific morning, I woke up and she was screaming "Get ready for school!" It was at least three hours early; maybe 4 or 5 am. It was snowing heavily outside. She was standing there, smashed drunk and high, in disgusting lingerie, boots and a leather trench coat. She could not even stand up straight. She walked outside in the snow and said "Let's go, NOW!" I was crying and terrified, trying to tell her it was freezing and to please put some clothes on. It wasn't near time to go to the babysitter's house and definitely not time for school! My efforts failed, she did not care! I was dressed ridiculously in high-water pants. I was ugly and nothing ever matched. I was always embarrassed and felt stupid. I got in the car and knew everything was all wrong! She was half-dressed, driving all over the roads, the snow was coming down heavily as she bypassed the babysitter's house and dumped me off on the school steps way too early. I sat there crying and freezing as she left and drove away. I did not know what to do. I beat on the school doors but no one ever came. She just drove away. I was so cold and I could not figure out why this was happening to me. I was just trying to get through the third grade! Hours later, the principal pulled up and saw me curled up, shivering and waiting on the steps. She let me in the door, sent me to class and no one suspected anything was wrong. I never told anyone because surely I did not want to be taken away from her, like she had told me, and put into foster care.

I was really beginning to hate my life more and more. I hated what I looked like – I was starving and skinny. I felt totally out of place. I knew something about me was terribly wrong. By now about the only memory I had left of "Mom" was the one dress I wore to church on Sunday's riding on the bus and I wore it to Janis and John's wedding. It was a "Holly Hobby – Little House On The Prairie dress" complete with an apron and bonnet that she had made me before she died on her sewing machine. "Mom" had really been proud of it and I loved it but now, I just looked ridiculous in the wedding. I really wanted and needed her to come back.

Day by day, I felt lonesome and more adult-minded as I became the caregiver for Janis. Her marriage to John was short-lived and he left. We were hungry and somehow she managed to go to work but made very little money. I always remember wanting food and being afraid of getting in the car with her. We called it "the booze wagon," it was a little red beat-up Gremlin with the floorboard full of trash, beer and whiskey bottles and cigarettes. When John was still there, she would occasionally make a meal but after he was gone, I just remember potato chip sandwiches, and the big jars of marshmallow fluff. One Christmas, there were no presents and we had bologna sandwiches. I remember the house being infested with fleas, jumping all over; I would get up on the kitchen table to try to get away from them and eat. I was always scared, anxious, hungry and cold. I was always fearful for her to wake up, wondering who would she be; the drunk one or the sober one? While she slept, I would clean up all the trash from the parties. I just wanted to get rid of all the empty bottles, cans, ashtrays and dust to see the table top. I

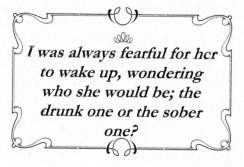

I was always fearful for her to wake up, wondering who she would be; the drunk one or the sober one?

wanted to clean all the stickiness off the floors and turn the music off. She would practically melt the records of Pink Floyd, Led Zeppelin, and Uriah Heep, playing them over and over all night and for days. It was never quiet and there was never peace. She became more and more dependent on alcohol and drugs and increasingly negligent and violent towards me. She liked to throw glasses of whiskey and then tell me to clean it up; "Mop it up brat!" she would scream, and then throw bottles of cleaner at my head. She would leave me with people she did not even know and stay out at bars all night. She would leave me with her friend's children and stay out all night. They would leave us alone with the oldest child in the house who was only eight or nine years old themselves. I was told that when I was two years old I was

45

given alcohol that made me drunk because the adults thought "it was funny". I just remember there being no food or any of the other "normal things" children should grow up with. Unfortunately, children of abuse; physical and sexual; will "play house" and abuse each other. One night I and three other children were locked in the car all night long while the adults were in a bar. Men were coming up to the car and I remember being very scared. When she left me somewhere, she would never let me sleep; she would come and wake me up in the middle of the night, plastered drunk and we would have to get in that "booze wagon." One specific night, we were in the car going under a bridge and she was hitting me and crying. She had run into my father at a bar, he must have been out on a short "break" from his life in prison. Apparently, he had been asking about me. She was angry and told me she would still be with him if it wasn't for me. During this incident the car door opened up as we struggled. I was being pushed and pulled while the car was in motion. Miraculously the door closed and my life was spared that night.

One evening my most frightening experiences happened. Janis picked me up in the middle of the night when we were out of town where her friends lived at the lake. They had been partying all night and left us at the house. She came to the door crying, angry and had blood flowing down her neck because her mouth had been split open. Her friend had punched her in the mouth while listening to a rock n' roll group called "KISS". Her friend did not like it and said it stood for "Knights In Satan's Service!" It was the middle of the night as she angrily forced me into the car. We drove for miles and she had no idea what she was doing or where she was going! I was praying silently in my head, scared and begging her to go back to that house. The next thing I knew, she was driving the car down a boat dock with a ramp and our car was headed straight down into the lake! I believe with all my heart that God intervened that night and turned that car around and we miraculously ended up back at her friend's parent's house where we slept overnight. I remember waking up that next morning, her friend and her Mom and kids were coloring Easter eggs. It was Easter morning! But I could not focus on the fact that it was a holiday; I was focused on what Janis would be like when she woke up. What would her mood be like? Sure enough, she woke up angry and sore from being punched in the face. Bruised and tearful, she was crying as she realized a poisonous, brown recluse spider had bitten her in the stomach overnight. She spent Easter at the hospital with a series of shots before we headed back to Kansas City. I will never forget that Easter Sunday.

Days, months and years passed…I don't really remember any fun or memorable times that I felt love, happiness or joy. I was always on edge, nervous, wondering what to expect next. Not only was there constant substance abuse, but sex was seemingly always around me, in front of me, and ultimately I was introduced to it in a variety of different ways. On three instances, I clearly remember going into a bar (for some reason it seemed permissible to allow children in bars in the 70's if food was being served) where a woman was dancing, topless, by a jukebox and on a stage. The adults would play strip poker all day and night and locked us outside of the apartment, with no one watching after us. I remember it being a very dirty, unpleasant apartment complex in Kansas City. I am sure it was a very dangerous area. We would just walk around for hours, hungry, and then beat on the door to ask for money so we could walk to a gas station to buy some snacks or soda. Her friends would answer the door, half-dressed, and throw us out some change. I remember pretending to be sick one particular night, making myself cough pretending to choke to convince her I was sick so we could go home, for fear of staying the night with her boyfriend, Eddie. It resulted in a ride home, with her in a drunken rage, screaming at me, swerving all over the road to get home. I never knew what to expect, day to day, hour to hour. I remember men being all around, taking advantage of her in her wasted state of mind. No one cared that I was right there, a small child, taking it all in; there was no escape!

When I was about eight years old, Janis had a boyfriend named Joe; how I hated and despised going there. He had a one bedroom studio apartment and a little boy, Larry, which he was raising alone. We would go there and Larry and I would sit for the entire weekend in a room and watch them and their friends drink gallons of whiskey, sending us kids across the street to 7Eleven to buy two liters of soda for their mixers and, if we were lucky, we would get some candy money for our dinner. They would get completely trashed and stoned. They would smoke marijuana and keep music blasting all night but just as his son and I would try to fall asleep, all the fighting and violence would start. She would end up with bruises, getting hit in the mouth with the telephone, earrings ripped out, blood on the carpet, screaming and crying – Joe would hide her car keys so she could not drive. I was glad for that but then the next day the entire ritual would start all over until the weekend was finally over. She truly was a form of a functioning alcoholic and had a good job working for the government; we would go home so she could get ready for the work week. During one of those weekend trips to Joe's, his cousin, named George, decided that he wanted to molest a child. I had fallen asleep on the sofa and woke up to this large predator pinning me down and hushing me to be quiet and I realized he had taken down my jeans. I was terrified and I could not move – I did not know what to do. I will not go into detail about this event but, I will say that it traumatized a little girl for <u>many</u> years.

"Wash Away Those Years" by *Creed*
She came calling one early morning
She showed her crown of thorns
She whispered softly to tell a story,
About how she had been wronged
As she lay lifeless, He stole her innocence
And this is how she carried on, This is how she carried on
Well, I guess she closed her eyes
And just imagined everything's alright
But she could not hide her tears
Because they wash away those years
They were sent to wash away those years

When he moved away from me, all I could think about was Joe's son lying in the floor in a sleeping bag. George was lying in the floor next to him purposely exposing himself. He was smiling an evil grin – in that moment I hated him!! I yelled for Larry to get up and rescued him, pulling him to the bedroom door where Joe and Janis were, beating on the door to please let us in. They did and just carried on. Looking back, as damaging as that night was, I thank my God that He was with me even then! Though that was a night of horrors, I believe there is a protective block in my memory of all the events that occurred. Little girls are not made for sex!! When I told her what had

I believe there is a protective block in my memory of all the events that occurred.

happened she was not hearing me and dismissed it. Not long after that, she allowed George to move in with us in our apartment!! He was always watching me, taking pictures of me with his Polaroid camera, talking sexually about our animals and saying sexual things to me as he lay under a blanket on our cheap, fake leather sofa. I think there are possibly things that I have somehow blocked out from that time and if so, I am thankful for that grace and mercy. For the next few years, we lived in that apartment in a low-rent project.

During this time, she and her husband, John, would be off and on. He would move in and out, fighting, partying, and unstable. Loneliness was a constant, daily friend but being alone was at least quiet and somewhat safe. I watched hours and hours of television, walked to school far away – all alone. I felt depressed and I was only in the fourth grade! I dreaded every weekend; the partying was overwhelming; it was so hard to sleep. I missed my "Mom!" I felt anxious; I was always cleaning, taking several baths daily, and checking locks on the doors. I would rearrange my entire bedroom with what little furniture I had at least once a week, color coordinating and hanging what few clothes I had and sought what little control I could have in my little life (likely the beginnings of Obsessive Compulsive Disorder.) I felt little, small and invisible. I know John, her husband felt sorry for me, but one day he could not take it all anymore and he packed up and was gone for good. The last memory I have of him was him trying to stop her from throwing a Mop and Glow bottle at my head as she was screaming for me to clean up her purposely broken glass of whiskey off the floor. He was done dealing with all of it and he had substance abuse problems of his own.

By now I was in fifth grade and my teacher at school began to suspect something was going on. One day, I had gotten a hall pass and I remember slowly limping as I walked to the girl's bathroom. After yet another incident of abuse, I was exhausted as I looked in the mirror and, lifting up my shirt, I pulled down the back of my jeans, revealing the belt marks. I had red belt marks with small circles imprinted all across my rear end and lower back. As I looked at them in the mirror, my friend Mary came out of the next stall, she looked frightened and asked me if I was okay. I started crying right there in the girl's bathroom and remember Mary hugging me before leaving me to go back to the fifth grade classroom. I was really tiny and pale. Janis had been drunk and had gotten angry about something. She was in a rage and demanded I take my pants down inside the apartment and bend over the black leather chair. I do recall it being a terrible beating with her 1970's metal ringed belt. I was screaming and begging her to STOP! I was shaking and could barely stand up. My friend Mary had been shocked by the aftermath I am sure. Most likely she had went back to class and I suspect made the teacher, Ms. Parker, aware of what she had seen. I remember Ms. Parker showing up at our apartment shortly after that. I had shown her our new kittens and I was terrified she would call

The teacher called and confronted my mother, but she told her everything was fine and to stay out of her business!

welfare, so I denied things because I had never heard anything good about foster care. The teacher called and confronted my mother but she told her everything was fine and to stay out of her business! We then moved back to my grandpa's house; the big empty house on Park Street where my only fond memories of "Mom" were before her death. When I was five years old, I remember one small birthday party in that house. "Mom" had a special brunette Barbie cake made for me with a blue dress that I will never forget. I never had another birthday party again until I was twenty seven years old, given by my husband, Rocky Candillo. I entered back into my first elementary school and now was in the sixth grade. I was back under the roof with two alcoholics again; my mother and grandfather. There was never peace! I began running away up to my Aunt Jan's house again, begging to stay with her. It just seemed like there was no escape for me, nowhere to run or find security. She cared for me but knew her hands were tied. I knew I was just going to have to SURVIVE!

A few other things that happened during that timeframe created even more anxiety for me. I had gotten somehow locked in a small bathroom at my Aunt's house and no one could hear me or find me. No matter how loud I screamed or banged on the door, it was no use. I was in there for hours…my cousin finally heard me and got a huge ladder up the side of the house and rescued me through the window. This incident has caused me great anxiety of small spaces and especially elevators in which I only will get in if there are other people and if I absolutely have to!

Another incident of abuse that happened that had caused a lasting effect is what I call spiritual abuse. One night we were at one of Janis' friend's house. Her friend's son and I were forced to watch a very popular, extremely demonic movie about possession. I was screaming and trying to hide behind her back, literally traumatized and frightened. We left and I was crying and was white as a sheet; while she was the last person that I would want to sleep with, I begged to sleep in the room with her. I continued sleeping in there for two weeks and she further traumatized me by repeating the movie, talking to me "in voices" and drawings of a demonic being naked, half man and half woman, with wings, were left lying around the house. The enemy had her mind held captive! He used every form of fear that he could to create fear and anxiety in me. But I was born with a purpose and a plan by God – I just did not know it yet!! She had me convinced that our house was haunted and she named the spirit "George" (the same name as the man who had molested me). For years I could never even talk about this because so much fear was planted inside of me. But now the truth has been revealed, *"For we don't fight against flesh and blood, but spiritual wickedness in high places – principalities in high places"* Ephesians 6:12. I have no idea why I had to endure those things – all I know is the Word of God is Truth, He makes us free and He had a great plan for my life and the adversary is defeated, *"Greater is He that's in me than he that's in the world!"* 1 John 4:4. The devil is a liar and has no power over a child of the Most High God, Jesus Christ!

I remember another time we were in a truck with a guy and the door flew open in a very busy intersection. My mother fell out of the truck, landing on her head and I flew flat on my back landing on concrete and ended up lying in the street with cars coming. The cars could have easily run over me but, I would assume again, Jesus must have dispatched an angel just for me. I remember being left by her, abandoned with people to babysit me that I did not even know, feeling unwanted. I do not remember any feelings of love or family, or any sense of belonging. I had no idea what it would be like to have a loving daddy or a mommy. *When my father and my mother forsake me, then the LORD will take me up. Psalm 27:10.* The next thing I knew there was talk of her joining the military and she was going to sign me over, giving all rights, to a married couple she knew! I did not need to be with this couple either! I could go on and on...about the abuse, neglect, and poverty but my intent for writing all of this is NOT to disrespect either one of my parents, but rather to reveal the "Redeeming Love" of Jesus Christ and His, and only His, transforming power in my life! His grace and unending mercy for me and you alike. All the episodes and trials and pain that I endured are real and if it relates to even one other person, drawing them nearer to Jesus then, just for one, it was all worth it.

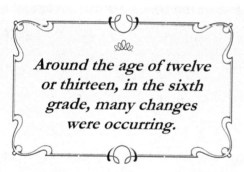

Around the age of twelve or thirteen, in the sixth grade, many changes were occurring.

Around the age of twelve or thirteen, in the sixth grade, many changes were occurring. A hormonal change during my teenage years was occurring and I was unaware of these changes in my body. I was lacking education, becoming very angry and tired of my situation. I was exhausted with my home life. I was sick of it! I began getting into trouble at school, disrespecting authority. My teachers did not know what was happening with me. I had picked up a couple of new girlfriends in the neighborhood and we began hanging out daily. I learned what make-up was, how to apply it and how to steal it because I did not have any money. We would go to the neighborhood stores and steal small stuff, make-up, beauty supplies, shirts, jewelry, etc. I started drinking; we stole alcohol, started smoking marijuana, and got in cars with boys we did not know. We were sneaking out of the house, running away on the weekends. I was listening to heavy metal music, attending rock concerts almost every weekend. My friend and I went to our first concert when I was in sixth grade, in the heart of Kansas City (Municipal Auditorium – Aldo Nova and Cheap Trick, my favorite songs by them were "Life Is Just a Fantasy" and "I Want You To Want Me"); we were alone and high. I was becoming totally out of control. I was hanging around all bad company. All of my friends sold drugs and they were making fun of me because I was a "virgin". They would tell me "just get it over with! It's cool!" I knew a lot of molestation had happened to me but I did not tell them about it. My friend's brother started coming on to us, he molested her (his sister) and me repeatedly. He was seventeen or eighteen years old. He would get us high and give us drugs. I thought I was in "LOVE" with him. My life made zero sense. My mother went to work each day and then got wasted every night. I was now running the streets freely by seventh grade. I did like how I looked now. I had a really cute body and a new face with make-up, a "mask". I was hungry…starving actually, for love, for food, for attention, for anyone to listen or care. Really just for someone to notice that I existed! My mother and I, by now, had a strange, turbulent and often volatile relationship; a strange "sister-like" connection, best described it. All I wanted was to get away from her. My friends and I would walk for miles or ride our bikes to fast food restaurants and flirt with and beg the guy at the counter for food and soda. We would play video games and just linger around, running around in the neighborhood and getting into trouble. Every chance I could get I would escape my home life. The craziness at my house made it easy for a troubled teenager to roam in self-destruction. My grandpa installed a pad lock on my bedroom door (that I had stolen from a school locker) to keep my mother out and cut down on the fighting. My room was now wallpapered with rock stars, like Ozzy Osbourne, AC/DC, Van Halen, Def Leppard, Aerosmith, Journey, and Poison. It was decorated with collections of bottles of the alcohol that my friends and I had partied away, and loud rock-n-roll music was always playing. I would invite my girlfriends over for the weekend and we would plan our weekend escape out the window! I began knotting sheets together one after the other to tie to the foot of my heaviest dresser and trail the other end out my window to hang down the side of the old two story house. We would get all dressed up in our rebellious style of clothes, piled on make-up and hair sprayed high! I would put the Ozzy album on, blasting "Crazy Train" to make her think we were in the room and out the window we would go! We would stay out all night long, in and out throughout the weekend. We would go to our favorite concerts, parties, hanging out with boys and parties at the lake. The sheet idea worked really well until one night when one unraveled and came loose. I flew down the sheet and my hand went through the glass window of the back porch. I explained the broken window with a lie; of course, and next I was on my search for a new way to escape.

We spotted a ladder on a neighbor's truck who was a painter. When night fell we stole the ladder and propped it up alongside of the house to my bedroom window. This method worked much easier, until one night we were too wasted to remember to hide the ladder in our shed when we were done. We went downstairs to get breakfast in the morning and there was Janis....staring out the back porch window through the kitchen, glaring at the tall standing ladder. She was so mad! In a rage, she stomped to the back of the house and pulled the ladder to the street curb for the trash man! She said she knew we were up to no good because of all the filthy, muddy jeans in the laundry. We would walk through the woods all around the lake; it

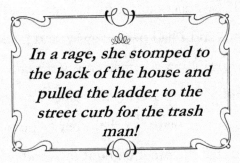

In a rage, she stomped to the back of the house and pulled the ladder to the street curb for the trash man!

was muddy and had been raining. We did not have a fear of the night. I had reached the point of little respect for her so what she said did not matter to me. She ripped the padlock off my door so I said, "Fine then, I'll just walk out the front door"!

When I was around 16 years old, during one of my routine rock concert weekend adventures I met a lead bassist band member who was quite famous at that time. Next, I found myself on a tour bus following him state to state attending his concerts. I ended up in another state not too far from home with no money and no way to actually get home. When I realized he was going to be traveling out of the country he decided to fly me back to Kansas City knowing that would be the best option. I was afraid of this idea, never even seeing an airplane before. I knew this was going to be my only way home; I had no one to call or to come and pick me up. I recall boarding the very small white airplane having no idea what to expect. I was scared yet trying not to show it and face embarrassment. I kissed him goodbye and headed for home. After arriving we talked on the phone a few times then he went on to make music and continue climbing the "wall of fame". After this experience my fears were tamed of flying. This made it easier for me to say yes to another poor decision of a future endeavor. I would later end up flying alone

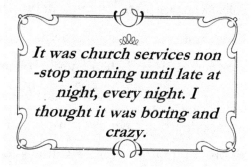

It was church services non-stop morning until late at night, every night. I thought it was boring and crazy.

to Las Vegas chasing dreams of my own "wall of fame".

During one week of the summer Janis's friend had asked me about going to a church camp with her daughter. I did not really want to go, but I thought about it. I did not really get a lot of invitations to go places; I was good friends with her daughter, so I decided to go. It was a Pentecostal camp in Westphalia, Missouri. I was in trouble immediately and told to go to the bathroom and wash my face. There was to be no make-up! I resorted to powder with a small amount of mascara and that did not even work. I felt ugly and bare. I was in the bathroom wondering why I came. I had to wear skirts or a dress to my ankle, no one else cut their hair, and you could have no contact with the opposite sex. Boys were on one side of the worship tent and girls on the other. It was the same way in the choir. There were very few limited breaks to eat and absolutely NO FUN! I went to find a phone in the cafeteria area and called Janis and her friend. I was crying and hollering stating that if someone did not come get me out of this culture shock I was going to run away! No one came for me. It was church services non-stop morning until late at night, every night. I thought it was boring and crazy. I did not understand why so many rules were in place. It most definitely painted a picture of a God of harsh rules, fear, and judgment! It was like I was in a time capsule in another world. I had never been around anything like this! I remember going into a big barn like area where there were many built in wooden bunk beds set in rows. I was on a top bunk. A bible was the first thing on the list of things to pack. I got mine out and started to flip through it. Even then, I knew God was real but I felt like He must have been so far away and for me, unreachable. I could not figure out why I was there and knew I could not leave. I figured I might as well settle in and survive the rest of the weekend. I was in shock at some of the religious behaviors that I witnessed there. Sitting on my bunk I realized one thing. I could hear the breeze outside, it was quiet there, and peaceful. There were rules, but there was also order and a schedule. I was not use to these things. I began questioning God. I cannot say that any miraculous things or changes happened to me, but when I left, "something" was different. I do recall coming home and going up the stairs to my small bedroom. There was Ozzy's poster on my wall, looking demonic as ever with long piercing fingernails reaching out with his hands and a multitude of others looking just as dark. I did not like the feeling that I was having that day. I got a big black trash bag and began unveiling the wallpaper covering every inch of the walls. I ripped and shredded all my rock stars posters one by one. Next, I gathered all the whiskey bottles and decorations that I had collected and threw them in the black trash bag as well. Though this was not the end of my rebellion it was a sign that a new awareness and thought process had been stirred up in the heart. Life presents many questions, challenges, struggles, and processes that lead to choices, decisions, and maturity.

Then one day when I was at the elementary school playground, I met these two little girls and they were so adorable and cute – the youngest one adored me immediately and asked if I could babysit them. They said their mother had been looking for a babysitter. They took me to meet her. She was so beautiful and friendly and very cool to me. Her name was Karen. She asked me if I had ever babysat before and if I liked to get high?! I said sure – I did want to babysit, her girls were so sweet and I always wanted kids. I always thought about what it would be like to have kids and how I would never put my children in the life that I had and they would never be around or exposed to the things that I had been exposed to.

However, Karen wanted to give me money to babysit and marijuana – Wow – I thought she was really cool! I was in junior high! She let me stay with them, she cooked food! She cleaned her house! She cared for her kids! She was beautiful and she let me have friends and boyfriends over when I babysat – she let me do whatever I wanted! I just could not believe she cooked meals, had dinner time…I did not care that she was on food stamps, welfare, drugs, and the cherry on top?…she was a former stripper and model, of course!! She introduced me to a whole lot of other nonsense – and we will just leave it at that. When a woman in her twenties is telling a twelve or thirteen year old child that they are best friends; sharing all of life's secrets, something is really dysfunctional. She was like a sister, mother, friend, role-model, and teacher – all that I never had. She just wanted to

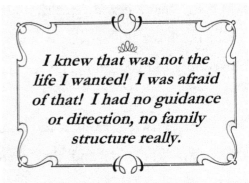

I knew that was not the life I wanted! I was afraid of that! I had no guidance or direction, no family structure really.

party and have fun all the time. I loved her and her family. She was also a deacon's daughter. Her family took me in, invited me to everything including church and it was all family-oriented. I stayed with Karen and the girls. My mother did not like it, but she was doing her own things too.

One particular weekend, my mother went out of town to the lake with her friends and I was under Karen's supervision. Karen was out partying that night and I went to the school playground to get high with a couple of guy friends that I knew. The next thing I knew, police sirens and lights were coming down the street, the cops were coming with flashlights, and one of the boys put a bag of weed in my shoe and threw it in the bushes. The officer pulled it out of the bush, and took me to jail. I was so scared; I sat in a yellow holding cell all night. I was fourteen years old, charged as a minor with possession, under the influence, and scheduled for a juvenile arraignment hearing. All night no one came for me. No one knew where I was. My mother was miles away at the lake, Karen was out somewhere, but God knew. Somehow, Karen figured out where to look for me; showed up at the police station and got me out of there. I knew that was not the life I wanted! I was afraid of that! I had no guidance or direction, no family structure really.

It was around this time that my Aunt Jan quit speaking to my mother. She could not deal with the stress of the situation any longer and soon after, we lost all contact with her. Karen and her girls and her parents were the closest family I now knew. I stayed with them a lot. Her parents even let me stay with them often. Whenever I would go back home, it just always seemed to turn in to a fight, a struggle. I was in trouble at school, skipping school, getting detentions, and there at home I was just angry and empty. When I was there, I would break things, destroy stuff; I just wanted to get away. I was drinking and getting high all the time. I felt like I did not belong or fit in anywhere. I just ran around with a bad crowd of friends constantly, partied and became increasingly promiscuous; searching for love in all the wrong places. When Karen moved, I moved with her, stayed awhile and would bounce back and forth from there to home. The struggles at home became impossible so my mom moved away from my grandpa, back into the apartment housing project and I was miserable. I was in my freshman year of high school. Everything seemed to be so difficult. I did not understand what I was supposed to do at the big high school, my schedule and I did not fit in. My life was totally and completely out of control and I was hungry! We did not have any money, I was so embarrassed, my mother signed me up for the "free lunch" line and I sat with all the "freaks" at lunch! I borrowed clothes from girlfriends, had big bleached hair and always high heels and boots. I did not look like a typical ninth grader. Not to mention my physical appearance was now very mature – I did not know what to do with all this. At fifteen, Karen and one of her friends decided I should try to be a model and I was approached to take pictures with a man that had photographed Karen's friend. He took me to his photography studio in an underground cave near Penn Valley in Kansas City and began shooting pictures. They suggested that I take some topless and get prepared so that when I turned eighteen, I could model for Playboy magazine. He told me I could never be any other type of "model" because I was too sexy. I was fifteen! I am pretty sure he may have drugged the drink he gave me because I do not remember a lot. I do remember going back there to view my pictures, alone. He could have raped, kidnapped or killed me – anything. I was alone with him in an underground cave in a dangerous area in Kansas City. All I can say is that God's hand of protection is mighty! I left there physically unharmed. My mind was flowing with modeling ideas and what I could do with that once I reached seventeen or eighteen. I met other men that did photography for me shortly after.

At fifteen years old, my focus was on ninth grade and then I saw "him"… surrounded by girls in the front of the school. His name was Tim. He was the football and wrestling star of the high school. He was very nice looking, appeared older, and came from a very wealthy family. He had my full attention at the first glance! Then I realized he was in my biology class! He was so nice and sweet and, of course, flirtatious. He was known as a "jock" and a "cowboy" and the most popular guy in school – every girl wanted him. I knew no amount of flirting would ever get him to want to go out with me. We were from two totally and completely different worlds and he was way out of my league. I knew he was too good for me. Still, in class, he always flirted and wanted to talk to me and I

As soon as I walked in the front door, there was my mother, drunk and throwing a bottle across the living room.

knew he had a girlfriend. For the duration of my freshman and sophomore years, I met another guy who had already graduated, was older than me and quite the partier. We had a steady, serious relationship but a lot of arguing. His name was Johnny. He kept me away from my house as much as possible and did encourage me to graduate high school. I thought I loved him but really did not know what I wanted except to escape my house and all the craziness that was going on there! One typical night, Johnny dropped me off to run in and get some clothes for school the next day. As soon as I walked in the front door, there was my mother, drunk and throwing a bottle across the living room. She really liked to throw them for some reason! It flew past me, broke on the wall, and then she kicked the coffee table across the living room. She was angry. Her friend was sitting in the kitchen, drunk, on the phone and crying; she was trying to cut her wrists! I was just trying to get some clothes!! I did not know what to do but hurried to get out of there. I remember snow falling – deep snow was on the ground. Janis, in her rose and stripe pajamas flung her trench coat on with leather boots and went out to her car, plastered and drove to the liquor store for more alcohol! I left. I just tried to stay away as much as possible.

Later, that next summer, something much unexpected happened; I was out with some girlfriends, and we were going to a party. It was a warm summer night. When we pulled up, I could hear music and people inside. There were some people partying outside as well and then I saw a familiar truck on the gravel road. It was Tim's truck. I remember that I was pretty drunk, walking toward the party, when he stepped out from the side of his truck and grabbed my arms and started pulling me to himself. He said he could not believe I showed up there and said he was so glad and that he always wanted to kiss me! I just remember kissing him a really long time…this was too good to be true – this could not be true!! Me, with HIM?! The next day I woke up and felt puzzled – was that a dream? That had to have been a dream!! Then the phone rang and it was Tim! I was in shock – it was real and he wanted to see me right away! I had some unfinished business though – I had been dating Johnny for over a year. I felt overwhelmed with guilt, but there was no way I could pass up my only chance to possibly go out with Tim! I called Johnny and broke up with him. I really hurt him. Tim came to pick me up and the first place he wanted to take me was to meet his parents! <u>ME</u>!! To meet his parents?! I had no idea what I even had to wear that could possibly be good enough! His parents were home builders in Kansas City and were in the Parade of Homes. He took me to meet them there. I did not know how to act, walk, talk; nothing! I had never been in homes like that! So beautiful!! I felt out of place! He said he'd thought about me for two years and was never going to let me go! I fell completely, head over heels in love with him. He proclaimed deep love for me. I was totally intoxicated with every single thing about him! I tried to change everything about myself, to be better, more like him and to hopefully keep him. I begged my mother to take me to Macy's Bargain Basement so I could try to get some cheap, normal clothes. I bought some dressy, preppy ones; some flat shoes, and dyed my hair back more brown closer to its natural state. I joined the pep club, the flag corps, and tried out to be a wrestlerette cheerleader for him! I did not make it. I just wanted to keep him forever. He made me feel different, others at school thought of me differently now. His parents were so kind and treated me with respect!? His home was like a mansion I had never seen before; he had everything! He would take me there every day after school and feed me, make me dinner, and we would be together for hours. I remember his parents being there and they were so accepting of me and our relationship?! They liked me!! He would turn up the music in the formal living room and spin me around and we would slow dance to Lionel Ritchie's "Deep River Woman", we could not take our eyes off each other. He changed many aspects of my life, how I felt about part of myself and I felt things with him and for him that I had never experienced in my life. We were young but in love. His parents took us to dinner plays and events…normal things. They went on a family ski trip to Colorado every year, at Christmas they invited me to go! I was so excited! I was around stable people for the first time in my life. I was a junior in high school, so was Tim. We went on the trip and had a blast! I had never been anywhere before! His dad helped me with ski lessons; we had fun! Tim was so loving and kind to me. I remember the most special moment, we were on the ski lift and he asked me to marry him. He said he wanted to get married after we graduated! We would kiss, he would always tell me that I was "the Queen of his heart", a song he used to sing to me. The rest

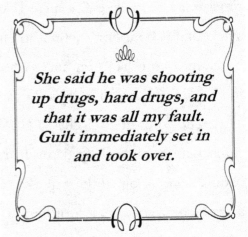

She said he was shooting up drugs, hard drugs, and that it was all my fault. Guilt immediately set in and took over.

of the trip was wonderful; I could not have felt happier. For once in my life, I was happy, on cloud nine and I did not care what was going on at home.

When we returned home, my mother decided to move again. Tim and I helped and we got moved into our first house. My mother bought it at a low cost from a friend – I hated it and was upset. It was in a terrible neighborhood and her friend's son used to deal drugs

68

from there. It was a known drug house. I did not like the decision but my focus was mainly on "my Tim." The next thing that I remember, I got a disturbing phone call. It was Johnny's mom. She said that her son was so upset over me breaking up with him that he had turned to drugs and was about to kill himself. She said he was shooting up drugs, hard drugs, and that it was all my fault. Guilt immediately set in and took over. I had a friend secretly take me to see Johnny. I was going to talk with him and see if I could help him and explain my feelings and let him know the seriousness between Tim and I that had developed and that was the direction my life was going. To deeply apologize and try to talk with him about the drugs, etc. The

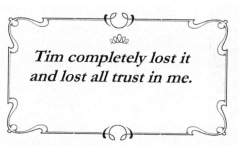

Tim completely lost it and lost all trust in me.

next day was one of my biggest nightmares and worst days of my life. My so-called "friend" called Tim and had told him that I had gone to visit Johnny. Tim completely lost it and lost all trust in me. He packed all of our pictures together, all my things in a black trash bag and brought it to school the next day. He was on fire. He broke up with me and there was <u>no</u> changing his mind; no going back. I was devastated, hysterical; I blew it! I should have never tried to help Johnny! I went to Tim begging and crying, on my knees, pleading for a second chance! He was closed and would not hear me. (Thank God that He is a God of second, third and 70 X 7 chances!) I knew it was over. This breakup crushed me, broke my heart in a million pieces and I was lost more than ever.

"Dead Flowers" by Miranda Lambert

I feel like the flowers in this vase
He just brought 'em home one day, "Ain't they beautiful?" he said
They been here in the kitchen and the waters turnin' gray
They're sittin' in the vase but now they're dead, dead flowers
I feel like this long string of lights
They lit up our whole house on Christmas Day
But now it's January and the bulbs are all burned out
But still they hang like dead flowers
He ain't feelin' anythin'
My love, my hurt or the sting of this rain
I am livin' in a hurricane
All he can say is, 'Man ain't it such a nice day?'
Yeah, yeah
I feel like the tires on this car
You said they won't go far but we're still rollin'
I look in the rear view and I see dead flowers in the yard
And that string of lights and it ain't glowin'
Like dead flowers, like dead flowers
He ain't feelin' anythin'
My love, my hurt or the sting of this rain
I am drivin' through a hurricane
All he can say is, "Man ain't it such a nice day?"
Hey, hey, I guess we'll just go to waste
Like dead flowers
Like dead flowers, dead flowers

I remember trying to drive my old, junky car away from his house. I was gasping for air, I could not breathe. I had lost the only good thing in my life, the love of my life, my heart. I can say this is the closest I ever felt to being suicidal. I drove hysterically to an old friend's house; reverting to my old self – searching for drugs to numb this intense pain. I found it; then I went to find Karen. I was in so much pain. I could not lift my head; I took total blame and guilt for the breakup. My prince was gone. All the next year, our senior year, he walked by me and anytime we came across each other, he would just look the other way as if he never knew me. I have never forgotten that relationship. It was so painful. I loved him with all of my heart. Before that senior year, I went back to stay with Karen and the girls. Karen had been going through some changes and she had been going to church. She invited me to go with her to a Michael W. Smith concert in Bonner Springs, Kansas. We went and we were in about the second row. It was there that God began to speak to my heart. I raised my hand to give my heart to Jesus, I did not fully understand everything, just that I felt something real. That following Sunday, Karen and her parents went to church. We told the pastor about the concert and I said I wanted to pray and be saved. This marked a very important event in my life. It was then that the seed had really been released and planted. I experienced a very real and authentic encounter with God. He showed Himself so real to me. This is what let me know He was real and this is what first built my faith. I confessed Jesus as Lord and Savior, but I asked God to prove it, show me...I wanted to ask for two requests. Number one, that He would deliver me from smoking marijuana, that I did not want to live this way any longer and, number two, that I could just meet my father at least one time. I wanted to see his face and know where I came from. My mother had told me that he was probably dead or in prison. I did not believe her. She said there was a possibility he was not the one. She knew he was but wanted to keep me from him. I had one picture of him on a motorcycle that I kept in my Bible for years. It is a very natural, normal, basic human desire to want to know your biological parents and heritage. I had searched for him for years, flipping through phone books, asking around of people who may have known him. I was so frustrated and angry with my mother and my life situation. I was trying to find him to see if I could run away to him and have a better life. I figured if he knew about me and where I was, surely he would want me and love me.

I prayed that Sunday morning, a very serious prayer and made my requests and plea to God. God is so real and so awesome and so revealing of Himself as we seek Him. With no exaggeration, I say that I was immediately delivered from the drug. I lost all desire to get high ever again; it was gone! I tested two puffs a few months down the road and threw up! It was clearly gone from me! That has been over twenty five years ago now and I have never touched it since! Praise God! Next, I went to school and I mentioned my dad's name to a girl at school. I had heard that her dad used to be good friends with him. The look on her face was one of shock; she said "Dana, someone else just came and asked me that same question." A younger boy, a freshman that I knew for a year or so, had also come to her that day. He had received a phone call, out of the blue, from a boy who we found out was our older brother who told him the truth of who his father was and he, in turn, came to school questioning the same circle of people I did. He called me that night, we were both shocked, we had been going to the same high school and now we find out we are brother and sister. Next, our older brother contacted me and shared some stories about our father and that we had a younger sister who lived in North Kansas City. He said he had pictures, lots of pictures, and he would share them with me if I wanted to meet him; I said yes! Then when I went to meet him at a convenience store down the way from me, I found that he lived only maybe one mile away from me all this time. It was crazy! The next day he took me north to meet my younger sister. She was a brunette and resembled me. Let me just say, all three of these other kids were in bad situations and lifestyles, which included drugs, drinking and my sister (who was probably around fourteen or fifteen) was already in trouble with the law. I had been made aware that she grew up, fell into drugs, sex trafficking, and was incarcerated and died in her thirties. We all went for a ride about 45 minutes away to meet our grandmother.

I cannot explain the strangeness of gaining an immediate family of siblings, along with more dysfunction. My grandmother did not have much to say to us but she did call me out over to her and told me that I could call her "grandma" because she saw her "son's eyes on me." That gave me a warm feeling. We left and drove home, I felt dazed and confused. Within a day or so, my phone rang; all of this happened within approximately a week and a half of my prayer! God did swiftly answer my prayer and proved to me His Power and Authority!! I answered the phone and Mr. McCartney's voice was speaking. He had a deep, powerful voice, yet spoke gentle words. He said "Is this my little darling? I know you are a doll..." I was completely speechless; I was crying, no words could come out and no words can express the wide array of emotions that were flowing through me. I could feel and sense through the phone who he was to me. It was real and finally, I had found him and he had found me. He wanted to meet us all as soon as possible! I learned he was a criminal (in prison). He said he was finishing approximately 15 - 17 years of hard time. He was close to being released. I was a young,

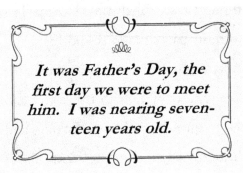

It was Father's Day, the first day we were to meet him. I was nearing seventeen years old.

naïve girl who just wanted a daddy – someone to care, love and protect me. The four of us piled in a car, our mothers sent a basket of food and we got a bottle of whiskey or two. We were all really nervous. We

headed for the prison – thank goodness it was in Missouri. Four young strangers uniquely bonded as siblings, all with different mothers. The dysfunction just kept raising the bar. We got to the prison. The other kids were dressed in jeans and tee shirts and no one had much money. I had on a turquoise fitted suit with a miniskirt and white high heels, my hair all done up big and a face full of make-up. I wanted to impress him; I wanted him to think I was pretty and want me to be his daughter. I was so empty. We approached the gate and the prison guard pointed to which one was our father. He was pacing like a caged animal. He had jeans and no shirt on. He waved to us. I brought him a special card with my picture in it and a poem that I had written for him. It was Father's Day, the first day we were to meet him. I was nearing seventeen years old. We were able to sit outside with him at a picnic table and we brought the food. It was a warm sunny day. We approached the table that he was walking to and I noticed that he was completely covered in tattoos; he said he had over 400. He was really muscular and his face was shocking to me because it looked just like mine. I could not stop staring at his facial features and I was very quiet and felt speechless. It was awkward. Most of the time we were there, I just looked at him. I now believe God granted me that gift that I did look so much like him, so that I knew who he was and did not have to wonder if he was for sure my father.

We stayed there for quite a few hours. My brothers and sister had a lot of questions for him. I just remember him saying over and over how sorry he was and that he loved us all and that he was about to be released and he wanted to start over and be a dad to us and have a relationship and he dreamed of getting a house where we could all visit him. As I said, I was young and naïve and I had no idea of the complexity of this man's life. I believe he had good intentions; I had already learned, up to this point, how devastating, serious drug and alcohol addictions were. However, drug addictions with a needle are a whole other story and level of problems. My heart was already broken and bleeding, Tim had crushed it, leaving it to almost nothing. I was filled with guilt and condemnation, a couple of the enemy's favorite tools. I hung on every word Mr. McCartney said and hoped as he got out, that soon my life would change for the better. I was trying to just make it to graduate high school.

My grandpa had given me a car; it was so beat up and ugly and old! It was a 1969 Buick Skylark with not a piece of straight metal on it. It did run, but I was so embarrassed that I would park at least two blocks from school and walk, even in the snow. I did not want anyone to see me in it. I had to beg for $2.00 for gas and $1.00 for a Taco Bell burrito from my mom and eat the free lunch at school. It was not a good feeling. To this day, I have no idea how I made it to graduation day. It was surely one of those times that Jesus carried me. I needed a plan and I needed money. I went to the school counselor and inquired about William Jewell College – I had always dreamed to go there. He kind of brushed me off and did not help me as he should have. I did not know how to pursue it or how to file an application and my mother surely did not either. I was seventeen now and I knew I should start pursuing that modeling career. Things were getting worse and worse at home; Janis was paying very little to no attention to me. Her alcoholism was intense and seemed unstoppable. When a person has gotten to the point that they are throwing up in bed and/or urinating on the edge of the bed thinking they are on the toilet; it is unbearable! Just before I graduated, one of my last memories in that house was a night that I came home late. She was sitting in the chair with a cigarette burning in her hand, passed out with head phones on, a Pink Floyd album spinning around; it was so hot it could melt. I never knew how she survived or did not burn the house down. But God knows because He had His Mighty, Marvelous Hand upon her too! I stopped the record and turned the music off and put the cigarette out. She flew out of the of the chair, going crazy on me. I went to my room and she followed, beating on my door and cussing, about to break it down. My friend had called and was on the phone and heard what was going on. He had sense enough to call the police. When the police came, she was enraged, cussing and spitting at them; it was either this time or a time prior that she pulled the officer's badge off. She was screaming at me, throwing alcohol, and came to the rocking chair where I was sitting, grabbed it and flipped it over with me in it. The police handcuffed her while lying on the floor. She was crying and I felt sorry for her. I wondered if she would ever hit rock-bottom. I felt like she hated me because of my father. The police escorted me to Karen's house where I felt safe. I stayed there as long as I could, all the while, trying to keep my grades up in order to graduate.

As graduation was soon approaching, I was out at a party one night. I was with a few people who were more like acquaintances than friends. I did not really have anywhere to go so I decided to just hang out with them and party for a while. There were a lot of kids there from my high school. I remember feeling lonely and like I did not really belong there and I recall an unsafe feeing. I stayed close to a really big foot-ball player that I knew, named Billy. We all sat in the living room for hours just hanging out; laughing as the guys were playing "beer games"-"Quarters"; to be exact. As I sat there on the couch that whole night, I could not help to notice, out of my peripheral vision a guy sitting by the bedroom door. We will call him James. James sat by the door as if he was guarding the doorway. He was calm, quiet and still. He bothered no one. I was informed that drugs were being dealt from the bedroom. People were shuffling in and out. The owner of the house, Greg; was a known drug dealer. We continued to party and I was becoming drunk. Later in the night there was a knock at the door and Greg answered the door. The front door aggressively swung open and a man proceeded to attack Greg, stabbing him at least 3 times in the chest! A fight broke out throughout the party. Another guy grabbed Greg and shoved him in a car, taking him straight to the Emergency Room. They were able to save him with approximately 10 minutes to spare. He had been stabbed in the lungs. Meanwhile, at the house, chaos was in full force! People were running and screaming everywhere. I remember another stabbing attack toward James. He was the man who had been quiet, minding his own business and guarding the bedroom door all night. I remember running out of the house and feeling like I had forgotten something inside. I recall crawling on the carpet, drunk and trying to find an earring that I had dropped. As I was on the floor, I noticed that James now was lying on the floor, on his back with his hands over his chest, saying "Help Me, Somebody Help Me"! I knew I could not help him and I was paralyzed with fear. Just then I heard Police sirens from the street outside and Billy came running in the house to look for me and he grabbed me and carried me out, I was terrified! I felt so sorry for James. Billy put me in his car. He then saw the attacker and got out of the car and was hollering at him and trying to fight him. Charles, the attacker, stood in the street waving the bloody knife. He had stabbed James in the heart that night and James, the quiet doorman died. Police were on the scene in minutes.

I went home very upset and shaken up! I told my mother what had happened. She was in shock that I would be at a party where something like that could happen. So was I! I was desensitized to chaos and dysfunction, but this was on another level. Many of my friends who were there that night were called upon as witnesses over the case. Justice was served, but this hopeless incident has been forever ingrained in my memory. (Do not be so deceived and misled! Evil companionships (communion, associations) corrupt and deprave good manners and morals and character. 1 Corinthians 15:33 AMP). There was so much going on during this time and so much uncertainty. My dad was released from prison and, as I stated before, I believed that he had good intentions and a good heart but the bottom line was that he was a drug addict,. He had a long rap sheet and he was not prepared for society. I think it is very difficult to fit back into society after being incarcerated that long. I was put in many situations that could have gotten me in a lot of trouble and I did not even realize some of the things that were happening. I quickly understood that I was not going to be able to run away and stay with my dad, nor would he be getting a house for us to visit. It was just on another rollercoaster of emotions with him. It was all really disappointing. One thing I can see is that God had His hand of protection on me so many times. I could have gotten into serious trouble at a young age. Even though I did smoke marijuana (before my encounter with God and my deliverance) I never had a desire for any hard drugs. I had an intense, strange, fear of them. I was around them a lot, but I am so thankful that I never became an addict. Every counselor I ever spoken to cannot believe that I am not a substance abuser or on medications. I am thankful for my Healer and my Physician – Jesus Christ! During this period in my life, I was going back and forth from my home to Karen's home. After this last incident with my mother, I moved everything I owned back into Karen's house. I was totally devastated by the outcome of my father's release. I had been going to church for about six months; I had accepted Jesus and I had faith; however, I did not get planted, discipled, and rooted. Psalm 1:3 did not happen; I was not "planted by the rivers of water to bring forth fruit in its season". I had it in my head, but not in the heart! Therefore, the magnitude of the situation with my father now along with my mother, graduation approaching, being poverty-stricken and having nowhere really to go, took a great toll on me.

I put on the lingerie and got ready.

Just as I had gotten all my things unpacked to stay at Karen's house, she broke her news to me that her husband expected rent money and knew that I did not have any so he really would love to accept the first month's rent by having sex with me. She said he wanted me for his birthday present! I could not believe what I was hearing; my heart was racing, what was I going to do now? I thought she was my best friend! She had lingerie prepared and asked me to put it on. I needed to graduate and figure out what to do next with my life, but I had to eat and have a place to stay. I put on the lingerie and got ready.

Then I realized that she expected to be part of this too! I was so upset and angry!! I took off running from the bedroom and called my Aunt Jan in desperation! I hadn't talked to her in years, but she was my only hope of family that may intervene. She came over to get me and said she was going to call the police if he bothered me again and to let me get all my things out. So, once again, I moved back to my mother's house. I felt like I was on a never-ending hamster wheel. I could not think straight and I certainly did not make good decisions; it was all about survival. I kept modeling for a little bit of money, but nothing was steady. I tried working at a fast-food restaurant and a clothing store. I was working hard on planning for that cap and gown. Karen helped me get a fake ID and I would sometimes go to bars in Westport on the weekends. Then I heard a commercial on the radio about a Miss Fox Hunt at Kansas City International Raceway. I had modeled, and also modeled semi-nude so I wondered how much this would pay and would it get me anywhere? I got some friends together and headed for the raceway. I entered the contest. There was approximately 45 – 50 girls signed up to compete. I was directed to a trailer to change my clothes and given a number to pin on my swimsuit; the trailer was full of girls. I changed into a little white bikini. I think the grand prize was around $300.00 or so, but the winner got to come back and compete the following week for a competition in Las Vegas. I really think I was there for fun and attention. I was just going to see what it was all about. I did not believe I would place. We all lined up in our high heels and walked out on the raceway; it felt really weird to be in front of that many people, staring.

The audience was really pumped up. The next thing I remember is being called out as part of the top three contestants and finally, I won the whole competition and was named Miss Fox Kansas City – I was stunned. They had me get in the back of a monster truck and stand and wave as it pulled me slowly all around the racetrack. It was a very strange and new feeling. The next week, they invited me to come back to compete in the Miss English Leather contest. If I won, they would send me to Las Vegas to compete there. So, I signed up. I took my winnings home and came back the following week. I got a new bikini and figured I had better start working on a tan. Some of the girls had told me about a new tanning salon (that is still in business today) that was really popular and had "the best beds." I called and set up appointments. Then I was ready to go, back to the Raceway, and try it again. It was the same scenario. More girls competing, but again I won the competition for Miss English Leather. Money and an all-expenses paid trip to Las Vegas to compete for the "Dream Girls Calendar" contest. I went home and told my mom that I was leaving for Las Vegas and not to worry. She did not like it. Las Vegas was not a place for a 17 year old girl to be flying out alone! This was a whole different ball game. Mom was right. There were at least 80 girls competing; these girls were not new to this profession! I saw a couple of their pictures in the lobby gift shop in adult magazines. One girl was on a billboard outside. We were each handed the same turquoise swimsuit, given instructions and a roommate. The competition was at a beautiful and grand hotel on the Las Vegas strip. We had to do swimsuit, bikini and evening gown; EVENING GOWN?!?

What was I going to do? I brought a prom dress that I had borrowed from a friend. These girls had very expensive, sequin dresses that draped down to the floor. They were seasoned at these competitions. I felt like I was just as pretty as they were and my body was in perfect shape but I was no match for their attire and experience. I was disappointed and did not feel I had a chance. I did not win this one. Looking back, I know God must have closed this door for a reason – who knows where it would have led me. Las Vegas is no friend to young, lonely and broken girls. I headed back to Kansas City. When I got home, I started locating any and every bikini contest in the city and signed up to compete. Then I learned I could make a little more by doing wet t-shirt contests; one thing kept leading to another. Then one day I headed to the tanning salon to work on my tan and I noticed some information and signup sheets on the wall of the salon. If a girl would sign up to show up at a certain bikini contest, there would be an entry fee paid just for showing up and competing; $75.00 - $100.00 just to show up? Then if you won the contest, you could receive another $200.00 -$300.00 more or the prize winnings. So, naturally, I signed up! The man at the front desk of the salon seemed really friendly. He began encouraging me to sign up and he would make sure that I got paid. He and his wife owned and managed the tanning salon. He just kept saying how pretty I was and that I should be able to win all of these contests. He was making money from the girls for just showing up. Meanwhile, I walked across the stage in my cap and gown and miraculously graduated high school. Even more miraculously, my mother and my father were actually at my graduation ceremony. I was very glad and very thankful to have them there. They both appeared sober. I graduated pretty close in order to Tim but he just walked by me like he had never known me, turning the knife in my heart brutally. The pain of losing him was sheer torture and unforgettable. I don't know that I will ever forget it. Up to this point, the progression of lies had built for my future. The next steps went from modeling, beauty contests, bikini contests, wet t-shirt contests, to the manager/owner of the tanning salon, pressuring me and calling me about becoming a stripper! I learned that he and his wife both "managed" dancers as well as a tanning salon. He ran a male group and his wife ran the girls! I could not believe it. I told him I thought I would be best just to stick with the contests because I did not think there was any way that I could ever do that! So next, the manipulator assigned me to a bikini contest at a bar. When I got there, I was paid and entered. I pinned my number on and walked out on the dance floor. Then I noticed something different, an applause meter. The emcee explained to me that this contest was different in the fact that judging was not just based on the judge's score but that you had to dance for the loudest applause from the audience! WOW – okay, well I was already in it at that point. So I danced and danced, I was nervous but determined to raise the roof with applause and shouting from the audience and take home the winnings. I did just that. The next day I called the tanning salon to grumble to JT about setting me up at a contest like that but I was in a good mood at the same time because I took home the cash! He proceeded to plead with me and try to sway me about the fact of how "easy" that was and that he knew I could do it and now all I needed to do was lose the top! He literally begged and pressured me, coercing me with compliments of how beautiful I was and what a "killer body" I had and that I would make "so much money", assuring me that I would be one of his top earners. He had "accounts" set up at all different bars in Missouri, Kansas, Nebraska, etc., primarily in the Midwest. He just kept calling my mother's house...I told him I was really unsure about it and that there was no way I could do this close to home – I did not want anyone to ever find out! He said it was no problem, which he would send me to Lincoln, Nebraska for my first time. He would not let up with his pressure tactics and manipulation. He had it all planned out and wanted me to drive my old, beat up car (no cell phone at that time) and go to Gladstone to pick up another 17 year old girl that he had "hired" and the two of us would drive to Lincoln where he had a hotel set up for us and scheduled us for a week at a strip club. I started to feel really uneasy about the decision and tried to back out and I told him I feared that my car would not make it that far. He just kept on pressuring saying that I would make thousands of dollars plus tips, in five days. I wanted a rental car, he said no. So I packed my suitcase and told my mother that I was going on another competition or to a modeling job. I was uncomfortable about my decision, concerned about my car's dependability but desperate for money and to find a way to make it on my own. With fear yet high hopes of making some fast cash in less than a week, I got in my old car and set off to follow JT's instructions. Under his influence and direction, I now feel (at that point) in my life I was being trafficked into the sex industry. These types of people know exactly what they are looking for to prey upon. They take a visual, personal, and environmental profile then groom and recruit the young lonely girl (or boy) who is promiscuously or loosely dressed, down and out, runaway, hungry, hurting and most likely already abused and/or abandoned. They are also looking for young, outgoing school/college aged girls who seem easy to entice with money and flashy things. Quickly they recruit and exploit her, whether it is into Strip Clubs, the Streets, or Sex Trafficking Rings. Sometimes by lure and entrapment, sometimes by force, drugs, and control. Either way they set her up for what seems an unbreakable bondage! My experience was 20+ years ago so I dare not imagine the snares and traps of today with such an advance in technology, social media, pornography, and the increase of perversion in society.

I had no idea of the door that I was about to open and the lifestyle that I was about to walk into. Life is all about choices and one thing is certain, when we separate ourselves from God

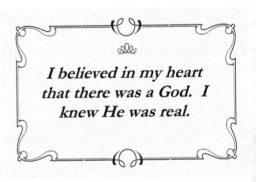

I believed in my heart that there was a God. I knew He was real.

it is because we choose to move. He never moves. He is always there. It is us who move away. I believed in my heart that there was a God. I knew He was real. I believed I was a Christian but I put myself first and my immediate needs. I did not fully trust Him. I had it in my head but not deep in my heart. I was still in control of my life.

I let my circumstances rule my decisions and because I was not firmly planted, it knocked me off my course. One bad decision can have a huge snowball effect that can cause much difficulty to recover from and usually follows with high price tags of consequences. I picked up a girl that I had never even met, named Teri. As I drove, I thought about the money and the reality of what if I drive all the way up there, committed, and cannot follow through with it? As I approached the Gladstone Apartment Complex, a pretty, young girl came out, the same age as me and unsure of what she was getting herself into. We jumped on the interstate and began our journey to Nebraska.

The Second Trimester

"Can anything ever separate us from Christ's love? Does it mean He no longer loves us if we have trouble or calamity, or are persecuted, or hungry, or destitute, or in danger, or threatened with death?"
~Romans 8:35 NLT

"Welcome to the Jungle" by *Guns'N Roses*

Welcome to the jungle, we take it day by day
If you want it you're gonna bleed but it's the price you pay
And you're a very sexy girl who's very hard to please
You can taste the bright lights but you won't get them for free

Welcome to the jungle it gets worse here everyday
You learn to live like an animal in the jungle where we play
If you got a hunger for what you see, you'll take it eventually
You can have anything you want but you better not take it from me

And when you're high you never
Ever want to come down
So down, sucked down, so down

"Simply Irresistible" by *Robert Palmer*

(1ˢᵗ song I ever danced to; Lincoln NE)

How can it be permissible,
She compromised my principle
That kind of love is mythical
She's anything but typical

She's a craze you'd endorse, she's a powerful force
You're obliged to conform when there's no other course
She used to look good to me, but now I find her
Simply irresistible, simply irresistible
She's so fine, there's no tellin' where the money went

1ˢᵗ song on stage for the 1ˢᵗ time – lie of the enemy

90

Chapter 2 - Survivor
Life as a Showgirl & Early Marriages

Little did I know that the road I was on would be the road I would stay on for the next seven and a half years of my life; a road to destruction, pure desensitization, and a lustful appetite for money that could <u>never</u> be satisfied. I lost what little of myself that I once had; I became someone else. This next chapter of my life is filled with a nightmare of regrets, and lost pieces of me that I can never regain. I am so thankful that my God, Jesus makes ALL things new! Without Him, I am nothing!

Teri and I drove and drove for miles, not really knowing where we were going. It was 1987-1988; we had no GPS or cell phones. All of a sudden, my car started jerking and jumping around. I can't remember if I had a flat tire but I remember pulling over and my car went completely dead; it would not turn over or start. We did not know what to do. We sat there for a few minutes and kept trying to start it with no luck. We got out and sat on the trunk for a few minutes to think - I was scared. There we were, two seventeen year old girls, stranded, on the way to danger; too naïve to know it. Now, we were in a very dangerous position because of a bad decision. Night was beginning to fall and cars were just racing by us, one after one. I got back in the car and tried again to start it. I remember it being hot outside and very muggy and for some odd reason my car windows were down a bit and the car was filling up with flies and bugs? It was definitely getting dark outside. We were about an hour and a half outside of Lincoln, Nebraska and I was beginning to panic on the inside. I told my new friend that I did not think we had an alternative but to hitchhike the rest of the way; I was terrified.

Teri flagged down a semi-truck and we reluctantly accepted a ride. I made her sit in the middle and I had my shaking hand on the door handle ready to fling it open at any time. I told her before we got in that if his hand moved even an inch toward her, I was opening the door and would not think twice about jumping out right in the middle of the freeway with him going 70mph. There was no way this man was going to rape me; I'd rather die first and I meant what I said. Again, my gracious God must have dispatched angels because we arrived in Lincoln safely and without harm. When we arrived at our hotel room, I thumbed through the phonebook to make an arrangement to tow my car the rest of the way and get it fixed so that at the end of the week, when I got paid, we could get back home.

We began to get ready for the night. We learned that the hotel room next to us had a few other girls that JT had "hired" staying there as well and we would all be going to work together that night. I was a nervous wreck. I remember arriving at the strip club and being unimpressed. It seemed to be in a bad part of town and the entrance was under a bridge, it was dark and very scary. We walked up a flight of stairs to the top where the strip club was located. I remember it being a very dark club with two stages lit up and the bar lit up. The bartender showed us to the dressing room. It was filthy! Not fit for an animal! I put my things down and a local girl, named Laura who was a fire dancer (she ate flames as part of her act) had just stepped off the stage and walked into the dressing room. She appeared older and rough, and she had handfuls of money (dollar bills) tucked all around her. It was then that I no longer cared what the dressing room looked like. I got dressed, primped and put on my stilettos. I went to the DJ's sound booth, picked out my first song, "Simply Irresistible" by Robert Palmer and my song list for the

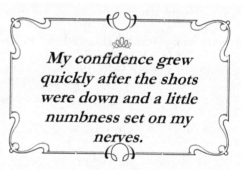

My confidence grew quickly after the shots were down and a little numbness set on my nerves.

night. I proceeded to the bar, made friends with Scotty, the bartender, who developed an immediate crush on me, and ordered two shots of Jack Daniels whiskey and an amaretto sour. I stared at the stage and the girl before me. I compared myself to her and watched and learned. My confidence grew quickly after the shots were down and a little numbness set on my nerves. The song started… "She's so fine…there's no tellin' where the money went…" the lights flashed, the song spun and my stilettos hit the floor for the first time. I looked at all the men with their empty, lustful eyes on me. I did not care about them, I did not like them, but a foreign confidence and new found power was in full force. Money was flying everywhere; I could not get to it fast enough! The enemy fed me the lie, that my body and my appearance was a cash cow and my key to success; I fell for it, hook-line-and-sinker! In that moment "Brittany" was born.

Brittany Foxx walked off the stage for the first time that night with around $70.00 in hand for six minutes worth of work! I was excited; I knew I had the whole night and several turns on two stages and a lot of money to be made. I ordered another amaretto sour and headed back to the dressing room to figure out a way to hide my money. I learned fast and worked all night. For me, and most girls, this job was not about sex or sexual feelings, but just the opposite; a dislike of men and a very serious game of power and control for once in my life and the benefit of gaining their money without dependence on them. The beautiful part was that they "could look but not touch!" I felt very powerful and for the first time, I was far from invisible and I existed in a new world, on a pedestal, admired and adored. I was constantly told how beautiful I was and complimented on my physical appearance. This attention was more than overwhelming and the complete opposite of what I was used to. I went home that first night with several hundred dollars. I could not believe the gold mine that I had found! I had no clue of the price tag attached to it. I had no idea of the years of tears, fears, anxiety, scars, distress and damage that it was going to eventually cause me.

The night before our final night there, the girls next door decided to throw a little party in their hotel room and they invited men over there. Teri and I did not go. We were tired and our bodies and feet ached. We were ready to go back home. We had one more night, pay day, then off to pick up my car from the shop and head back to Kansas City. We had nothing to do with what went on in the next room. In the morning, we learned everyone over there was passed out with hangovers, the men were gone and their hotel room was totally trashed! Alcohol, cigarettes, food, trash all over the room, things broken and light fixtures ripped out of the walls. Teri and I

He took every dime, showing us "he was in <u>control</u>"!

packed our suitcases and checked out and headed to work for our last night. Just as we were coming to the bar at closing time to get our weekly "base pay", we noticed JT standing there with his wife. He was on fire, mad! He had driven all the way from Kansas City, overnight to come up there and take ALL of our money! He took everything from all of us and said he had to pay for all the hotel damage and he did not care if Teri and I were not involved! I was crying and pleading with him but he was cold hearted and did not care. He took every dime, showing us "he was in <u>control</u>"! Thankfully I was able to pay for my car with the tips that I had made but, instead of going home with several thousands of dollars, I wound up going home with under $500.00!! I was very angry! This was so unfair and definitely not right! But what was I going to do about it, call the police? Obviously not! He just told me too bad, don't worry about it, that I would make it up the next week at the next "great job" he was sending me to! What choice did I have now? We drove home to Kansas City. I was upset and I knew there was nothing I could do about what just happened. I felt powerless. From the start, I should have recognized (my first experience) that I should have run from getting involved in this lifestyle, but I did not.

I grumbled all the way home. Even though he took my money, I still had my tips and that was enough to eat for a couple of weeks and put gas in my car. I thought at the time that it was easy money. I'd gotten past the fear and desensitization had already set in. I worked for a couple more weeks for JT at several different clubs in Kansas. The other girls talked about the male strippers who also worked under JT all the time. Some of them went to watch them dance on their night off. I kept hearing about "the favorite," best male stripper around named "Blackie." JT's wife used to date him and they were going on and on about how he was going to fall in love with Brittany when he saw her. I just laughed and passed them off.

The next time JT scheduled us to dance was in a club in Junction City, Kansas. I was nervous; I was told this was nothing like the club in Nebraska or where I'd been. This club was very big and upon entrance, to the right, was a separate bar and dance floor for the male show and to the left of the entrance, a bar for the female show. The stages were large and grand, lights and mirrors everywhere, and different levels of plush seating. Mostly I remember a lot of bars and poles. Prior to going there, we were instructed to meet and carpool with the other dancers at the toll gate entering the Kansas Interstate.

When we got there, we met other girls and a couple of cars full of the male strippers. That's when I met Blackie – he came over and started talking to me and telling me about where we were headed. I was scared and excited all at the same time. When we got to the club, females separated from the males and we all made our way to the different dressing rooms. When it was my turn, I made my way to a huge stage where it seemed like a million eyes were on me. When I glanced back toward the dressing room, I noticed Blackie had come over to our side and was standing still and staring at me working the stage. When I finished, I went to the dressing room and he was gone. The girls were excited and throwing on clothes over their costumes, asking me if I wanted to go with them across the hall to watch the male revue. We could go in between sets when it wasn't our turn to be on the stage. So we went. Blackie came out on the dance floor. I am sure my mouth was open and hanging to the floor. He was by far the most beautiful man I had ever seen or been around. He came out with a Zorro type mask on, his hair was long and full, his eyes were a piercing blue-green and he had a model face, his body was literally chiseled and perfect. He was super tan and wore black leather pants with boots and bow ties. He was most definitely the boss and in charge and he was the person JT always put in charge. I could not stop staring at how good looking he was; I turned to one of the girls and said "I am going to marry him!" It sounds crazy, I know, but I seriously meant it.

When our shows were over, he asked if he could ride back to Kansas

City in our car with us. He wanted to sit in the back seat with me. I was mesmerized by him. There was definitely a connection between us. He kissed me all the way home to KC. I remember going home to my mother's house that night and hanging his poster on my bedroom door. He was front and center with the group name, "BODY HEAT", printed across them. I was on a high. I thought to myself "Now I might be able to get over Tim!" Little did I know that I should have turned and ran for my life! I thought that I had problems and an abusive past but all hell was about to break loose in my life! I was still a teenager, just out of high school turning eighteen and headed into the darkest days of my life.

Blackie called me the next day and said that he had a girl living with him, but he was kicking her out that day because he had to have me. He wanted me to come over that night because he said he would have her out before nightfall. I did not care, I just wanted to see him again and be seen with him. I went that night to his apartment. He and his friends were getting high. I told him I'd pass that I did not get high anymore. His friends all left and just after they did, the girl showed up saying she wanted the few clothes she left behind. I went in the bathroom and shut the door. I heard screaming and crying and the door slam. I did not see what actually happened but the girl had a terrible black eye because she was seen by all the people we knew over the next few days. He said the door hit her as they were arguing and he was trying to shut the door. This should have been a clue to me that I would be next and to go home! I never went back home...

except to get my clothes and belongings to stay with him. I knew neither of my parents were going to take care of me and besides, I knew how to make money now. I made more money than Blackie! Female dancers generally always make more money than male dancers.

Two or three days after I met him, Blackie's mother passed away in Oklahoma. He was a complete basket case! I got on a plane with this man that I had just met to go to his mother's funeral with him. Again, after this short trip I should have ran with lightning speed but I did not. Dysfunction and abuse were no strangers to me and his family was full of dysfunction. His father was an Assembly of God preacher. He and Blackie's stepmom loved me immediately because I told them I was a believer and had gotten saved at an Assembly of God church. Jimmy Swaggart was loud and clear on their TV set the whole time I was there. I later was told by him that his mother, who had passed away, was his step-mother's sister and that she had molested and abused the boys. Blackie was a mess and I felt sorry for him.

When we went to his family's house that night, it was obvious that they were hoarders; you could barely walk through the house. As we sat there, his eyes glazed over with sadness, he quietly pointed to a little boy across the room that was approximately 5 years old. He shared with me that the boy was his son and that the little boy's mother was Blackie's cousin! I was so confused and did not know what to think. He said his cousin threatened him that if he did not have sex with her that she would tell her dad, his uncle, that he had raped her. I was naïve and believed it and besides, I was focused on his mother's funeral so I somehow passed it off. I am sure I wanted to ignore that information. By looking at the exterior, I would never have guessed how messed up the interior of Blackie was, and believe me it was bad. We were both on the run from our God and the truth. We both knew about God and believed but we wanted to live life our own way and the mask was easier. The funeral was super emotional and after it was over we flew back to Kansas City. I remember looking at him in the airport and I could not believe he was "mine" and that we were together. In our circle of friends and work, I was proud to be with him. As soon as we got home he wanted to go over to his friend's apartment across the street; a fellow dancer named Sampson, who was getting ready to leave KC and start working with the Chippendales. We went over to visit and as I was sitting there, all of a sudden, the two of them began doing lines of cocaine. WOW! I was stunned. I said "No thank you – I don't do drugs." I waited until we got back to our apartment to tell him that if that is what he was all about, it was not going to work out between us because (for some reason) I was against drugs and I was very scared of hard drugs. I had seen the damage they had done to both of my parents, especially my father. He assured me that I had nothing to worry about, that he was just testing it and he only sold a small amount each month to pay his rent and all the money he made dancing was play money. This guy could tell me that the sky was yellow and not blue and I would have listened to him.

During this time, we were both dancing, making money and had become top earners - literally a dream team boyfriend and girlfriend. We had talked of getting married in September of 1989 and we both had a deep desire to have children. He was five years older than me. We had a deal that when we were working, we did not go to the shows and watch each other because it was too hard and caused jealousy. At the same time, we both could handle the fact of what the job was because we both knew it was about power and money. However, this is true for the female and men tend to get turned on and single women out to mess around with after the shows. He was cheating on me. He was doing drugs. He was injecting steroids and doing cocaine. This was not a good combination for an angry guy who had a well known background and pattern of abusing women. It wasn't long before he began abusing me. He would tell me that I was pale and bruised easily and that he did not really hurt me. He would rip my clothes off – even in public – he did not care. He got banned from several bars for fighting men and fighting with me and he would tear up bars; even tear doors off bathroom stalls in the ladies room, trying to get to me. He tore our cars up – everything, you name it.

Eventually I told him that I was going to get a house and take a break. I was also still modeling and I was taking pictures to send off to Playboy to try to get in the magazine and he was contemplating going with Sampson to work with the Chippendales. He used that as leverage. He liked the idea of me being in Playboy but at the same time he did not like it, so he said if I was going this route, then he was leaving with Sampson out of state. I was torn on letting him go or getting married. I found a house and rented it and told him I was moving and he could think about what he really wanted but that the abuse needed to stop. Within two weeks, he had moved into the house with me but unfortunately, the abuse never stopped. Almost all of the bills were in my name, I paid the majority of the bills, and he was getting heavier into drug use and dealing. We were fighting and the abuse was horrible. He and my best friend's husband started talking about doing a big deal and making a ton of money. I wanted nothing to do with any of this. I begged him not to do it but he wouldn't listen. He had gone behind my back and brought a large quantity of cocaine in my house in coffee grounds and hid it in a ceiling appliance. He could've got me in trouble and I had no part of drugs. He started bringing strangers in my house and would tell me to just stay away or upstairs, that these men were doctors who were wealthy and they wanted to test it and they were behind the deal. I was so furious with him. I pleaded with him, I knew he was being set up, it was obvious, but when drugs have a hold of you, nothing seems to matter. I told him he was going to get busted. I woke up one morning and he was gone in <u>my car!!</u> I had a sick feeling in my stomach. Sure enough, he called me a couple of hours later, my car was impounded and he was in jail. He was crying like a baby. The "doctors" were really the DEA and Blackie was busted for selling approximately two and a half kilos of cocaine straight to them! Strangely, a few hours later they brought him home. He said they wanted him to work with them and he said he would cooperate because he was facing a ten to twelve year sentence. I did not know what to think or do. He proceeded to tell me that they wanted him to wear a "wire tap" and go undercover. I was scared but I needed to go to work – someone had to pay these bills.

Two days after he got busted I found out that I was pregnant! My emotions were all over the place. I was happy about the pregnancy and so was he, but we both lived in a fantasy world. I was young! I had just turned nineteen and he wanted to get married right away. I was confused! I said we should wait and see what his sentence was and get married after he got out. I really did not want to get married at this point because I knew he would be leaving for a long time and he was abusive, to say the least! He wanted to up the date and get married in July. I was wavering, then he said the magic, manipulating and hurtful words that contained a powerful hook of pain, fear, and shame. He said "If you don't marry me now before I leave then I will not have anything to do with you or the baby and the baby will not have my name!" That ripped my heart in half and pierced the greatest fear that I had… that my child will relive my childhood and be born and raised fatherless!! There was nothing about my childhood or the depth of pain in my heart that I could ever allow or bear to happen to my children. I was always determined to do the exact opposite and give my kids what I never had. We were joined in marriage in July. It rained and poured and stormed the entire day. We were married at an Assembly of God church in Kansas. I must say the wedding of "Brittany & Blackie" was quite a spectacle. Lined all across the platform were men and women who were all adult entertainers. The entire bridal party was comprised of strippers – male and female. There were possibly only a couple of people who were not.

One of his arrogant friends smarted off and said that maybe the weather outside was indicative of the day. Karen's father, who was now a minister, performed the ceremony. My grandfather walked me down and gave me away. As I joined Blackie, we turned to look at each other while the song "Endless Love" by Diana Ross played. We were both emotional and I had a million things on my mind. I was young, tired and newly pregnant. I was worried about his sentencing and, although he looked magnificent in his tuxedo, looking at his face, I could see that it was full of make-up, concealer that is. Both of his eyes were black and blue. He had gone out partying the night before our wedding and gotten into a fist fight. I was very upset that morning when I saw him. Would the chaos ever stop? How can a marriage be real if both people are stripping for money? However, I can say that this was a common thread in many people we knew; strippers dating and marrying strippers. To this day I don't know of anyone that their marriage lasted.

When the wedding was over, there was no honeymoon; not one of destination or emotion. Daily life and thoughts circled around money, the pregnancy and him being in a lot of trouble with the law. Close to this time we had outsmarted JT and taken over the management through bar scheduling. Blackie and I were known all over. We had a good rapport with many bar owners and they knew we would show up and bring a following; anyone who wanted to work hung around us. We changed the name to Elite Male and Elite Ladies of Kansas City. We worked primarily in Kansas and Missouri but other Midwest states as well. I was feeling tired and wanted to make some quick cash because I needed nursery furniture. As I had just found out that I was pregnant, I knew my time was running very short to make money. My best friend, Shelly, and I decided to sign on

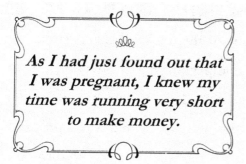

As I had just found out that I was pregnant, I knew my time was running very short to make money.

for a week-long job at a bar in South Dakota to make some quick cash. This was a particularly dangerous and degrading experience. We boarded a Greyhound bus and had no idea how long of a ride we were in for! It seemed like forever on that bus, night fell and it became dark. I began to feel scared as we arrived at an Omaha bus stop in the middle of the night. I knew this was not an okay place for us to be. We waited for quite a while for the next bus to arrive, got our tickets and boarded again. When we arrived at our final destination, we quickly knew something was wrong. It was night time, a bad area and we did not know where to go or what to do. We were standing on the side of the street. Someone was supposed to meet us at the bus stop, as I recall, but no one was there. We were scared. We found a pay phone and called the bar, attempting to find a ride and our destination to stay for the night. There was no hotel booked and I was fragile, nineteen and pregnant. All of a sudden, a guy pulled up who knew us and said he had the key to the house where we were supposed to stay for the week. He dropped us off, gave us the key and gave us directions to get to the bar. We were to work the next night.

When we entered the house, it was FILTHY AND DISGUSTING!! There were three twin beds and one of them was already occupied by a girl from Minneapolis. She was complaining about how horrible the house was. We did not know what to do! We did not know our whereabouts, had never travelled here and just figured it was probably safe and were going to stick it out for the week. It was so dirty, the refrigerator smelled of moldy, nasty food that other girls had left, the beds were dirty, and we were scared to death of the toilet and the bathtub especially! Shelly bleached the bathroom thoroughly, scrubbing before we could even think of bathing! This was a house that the bar had set up for the out-of-town girls. I was appalled. However, there were thousands of dollars to be made fast so I kicked back on the twin bed with my book full of baby names. With scared and happy thoughts about being a momma for the first time, once again, the feeling of numbness and desensitization set in. I just needed to get through this week, make a ton of cash and get back on the Greyhound bus for Kansas City! Next, I figured up the months and thought I could enter the Miss Budweiser contest in Kansas City before I started showing. It went on for several weeks and I won in the first week. I then needed to wait for a few weeks so that, at the end, for the final competition, each girl who won weekly could enter to win the title. The final week I was definitely feeling pregnant, but not showing yet. I was about five and a half months along. I had a custom made white swimsuit with rhinestones, long red fingernails, and sparkling silver stilettos and sprayed on three bottles of spray tan. The audience and judges were going crazy! There were a lot of people there – one of the main judges is currently still the owner of one of the strip clubs that we minister in today! No one knew or could tell that I was pregnant. I won the entire competition and the title. The judge came up, told me that I was super sexy and classy, and presented me with a big diamond ring, an all-expenses-paid trip to Las Vegas and $1,000 in cash. I was so excited; I just wanted to furnish my baby's nursery. After all the pictures and hype, the judges learned that I was pregnant; they were stunned and shocked, hugged me and wished me luck. My pictures were hung all over this club as well as some others. I had posters up at Country Rock for their Miss Tight Jeans contest.

With my modeling and Playboy plans now put on hold (thank God He intervened!), times got harder because now I was out of work; Blackie was dancing a lot but did not make the income that I made. I can't imagine what the neighbors thought – he had probably eight to ten male dancers at my house every week for practice. They would take music and do all their routines in my front yard, on a busy street with cars honking and passing by. They choreographed everything – as we did with the girls too. There were things about the lifestyle that were fun. *Sin is fun...only lasts for a season then the misery follows...* Blackie grew increasingly angry and nervous due to the fact that he was constantly being called by the DEA to wire up and go undercover to meet drug dealers. I spent my entire pregnancy worrying all the time; every time he walked out the door I was nervous. We moved out of the house into an apartment and not many knew where we had moved for that very reason.

One time he was ordered to go undercover, he wanted me to go with him. He was wired, these were big time dealers and the DEA wanted to move in on them. He wanted me to go because he thought if something went down they would be more merciful. I remember wanting to get out of there. It was an apartment, a lot of drugs, a large safe, three or four Hispanic guys and a girl and at least one gun on the table. They knew I knew nothing and wasn't involved; I was just there and quiet. God must have been there right next to me because we left quietly. That whole operation went down; that was a major drug bust and was on TV. Years later, I visited one of the main men in prison to plead safety over my daughter and myself. I knew the word was out hot and heavy on Blackie and at that time, he was in another prison for protection. While we stayed in the apartment, he was seriously abusing drugs and steroids. He was a very violent person and violent towards me. Several abusive things went on during that time that I will not discuss out of respect for my oldest daughter. His time was running out. During my whole pregnancy and the next year during the first year of our daughter's life, he was on borrowed time, working with the Feds. He was partying constantly, cheating on me, and facing time.

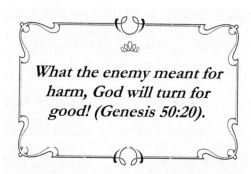

What the enemy meant for harm, God will turn for good! (Genesis 50:20).

My beautiful daughter was born in February. She was flawless and perfect. He loved her greatly and was a good daddy to her but he was jealous over my bond with her. He wanted to feed her a bottle so he refused to allow me to nurse her. He knew he needed me to get back to work as well. During that winter, our electricity was shut off and we had no heat. He needed me back in operation. Two weeks after I had my daughter, I was back on the dance floor. I had only gained eighteen pounds during my pregnancy so I did not have much to lose as I left the hospital. I was back in full force, calling girls to go with me and scheduling. It's funny now that God is using my past to do ministry in a similar manner, such as scheduling, planning and taking women with me monthly, only now, to minister to the girls in the clubs! What the enemy meant for harm, God will turn for good! (Genesis 50:20).

As I knew Blackie was nearing the time of turning himself in to do his prison time, so many things were going crazy. I knew he was partying hard; he would not come home after work and he would routinely head to the bars in Westport and I would go on relentless chases to try to find him and catch him cheating. He would insist that I go home and stay away from him. He was an absolute train wreck!! He was abusing steroids, doing cocaine, drinking hard liquor. You name it, he was doing it. He knew his freedom was running out. He was violent and always starting trouble. One night, I was looking for him; I was at a popular club on the corner in Westport. As time passed, he and all his entourage came barreling through the door. When he walked in, everyone knew that he was there. He commanded attention. Everyone knew him and women flocked all around him. He saw me and was angry that I was there, telling me to go home. Next came the normal scene – he got into an argument with a guy and a fight broke out in the middle of the club. I saw chairs flying and him breaking a beer bottle, and then he was standing up tall on a chair, in the middle of the room. He looked so good, all tan, beautiful hair, buff body, in a silk, purple, unbuttoned shirt – all eyes on him....stunning and CRAZY, eating glass from the broken bottle and spitting blood on the guy, saying he would kill him! Suddenly, he was surrounded by bouncers, dragging him out and banning him from the club! (This was a very typical scenario that happened frequently.)

I remember sitting alone at the bar crying. I was very drunk. I took my contacts out of my eyes and had them in my hands and laid my head down on the bar. Just then a girl named Sydney, who I danced with and worked together with, came up and said hi to me. I closed my eyes on the bar and passed out. Sydney and her friend carried me out of the bar. (Angels must have been encamped all around) I did not know Sydney that well but I was thankful for her that next morning. I remember waking up in a fetal position, my ankles burning like they were on fire, and I was curled up with my face lying against a concrete floor of a very small, strange bathroom! I did not know where I was. I got up and realized that I was not wearing my clothes but I had someone else's clothes on; sweats that were too small and the elastic bands were about to cut the circulation off from my ankles. Then Sydney appeared to check on me. She told me that she helped change my clothes so I could be more comfortable. I remember lying in the bathroom floor and all of a sudden Blackie showed up, carried me out of the bathroom and her house and thanked her. The time was short and intense and nearing for him to leave us for prison.

On another night, my friend Misty and I went to work at one of the clubs we now minister in and we went back to the dressing room. Two girls we did not know were sitting in the room talking. As we entered, the girls were talking about how they had been at the Elite Male show the night before and how they had "entertained" Blackie and Ice Man after the show. They had no idea they were talking about our husbands! I was so angry! We began questioning and arguing with these girls. I threatened one and told her to leave the club with me immediately to go and confront Blackie. "Leave your good customer for the night or it's gonna be bad for you!" I was ready to fight her. I knew he was about to leave for years and I wanted to confront and catch him cheating, as if, at this point, I needed justification to leave and divorce him. We drove straight to Westport, walked into Lyn Dickey's and there he was, sitting with his arms around two women! We walked right up to them. He knew I was on fire! I asked him if the girl I was with looked familiar from the night before. He flew from his chair, told the girl she was crazy, spitting in her face, calling her a whore. Then he chased me as I ran into the ladies room – he came in and ripped the stall door off, I was crying. Again, we were banned from another club. I knew the girls' details of the night before were true. If he wouldn't have gone to prison, I have no idea how I would've gotten away from this abusive relationship. Every day and every night leading up to his surrender was a NIGHTMARE – the physical and emotional abuse was beyond overwhelming.

I wish I could say that the abuse and terror stopped but it never did. He moved us back into my mother's house as he was drawing close to incarceration; he thought we'd be safer there. Even though I knew in my heart that he was cheating, I could not fully prove it. I did not want to wait for years for someone if that was true. So next I put a tap on my mother's phone. I caught him on recording within two days with three other women. He came walking in late one night and the recording was playing, I locked my mom and the baby in the bedroom and called 911 before he walked in. He went crazy, breaking lamps, etc., and I told him he needed to leave and go stay the duration of his freedom at a friend's house, that the police were on their way. I knew how he would react to me knowing the truth. He left, we talked on the phone, next in public and at a park and then his time out was up. He had worked enough for the DEA to get his time reduced from ten to twelve years to just four and a half years. He was scheduled for Federal Indictment. I remember going before the Federal Court and thinking how scared he must have been. He wanted the baby and I to be with him. He thought the judge would be more merciful. I am so thankful that when we really blow it, God is a God of second chances! Actually seventy times seven and I am so thankful to be under His grace and mercy!!

The following year in February, we drove to the federal penitentiary. He had one of his friends drive us because I knew I would be too upset. Even though our marriage was a ton of dysfunction and abuse, it was one of the hardest days of my life. We pulled up to the gate with our baby in her car seat and he kissed her as he got out. He was an emotional wreck but I can say he did face it like a man and surrendered himself; he did not run. I had purchased him a Bible and I put it in his hand and he walked through the gates, holding nothing else. As we drove away, my mind was racing with thoughts. As dysfunctional as it was, I took my marriage to him very seriously. I had been abused in a thousand ways, stabbed in the back, cheated on, spit on, and abandoned. I knew I had a great responsibility on me now. I had a daughter that I vowed would never have a life like mine. I vowed that she would never see me with a drink in my hand and never be in a car with me under the influence of alcohol or drugs. To this day, my children have never experienced that kind of lifestyle. They do not know me in any other fashion but a Christian woman. My God is a Redeemer of the lost! He is awesome and powerful. I knew I had to take care of my child on my own. How was I going to get out of my mother's house? I got home, pushed myself into "survival overdrive" and worked every night to quickly move out on my own. I had just turned twenty one and temptation was all around me. I did not want to be married to someone I could not trust and who was abusive. I had had enough! I had boyfriends. I was dating, but I never brought men to live in my house around my child. There was never alcohol or any other types of influences in my house when my daughter was present. I was a protective momma bear like no other. My daughter was well taken care of. I was, and am, an over-compensator – her every need and most wants were met. I was working a lot. I had told my mother that the only way she would ever have anything to do with my children was if no smoking and no alcohol were involved. Something had begun to happen within her. She started locking herself in her room and "sweating it out." She had been going to church! I saw a difference in her and her behavior. She began babysitting my daughter at night while I worked. For the next few years I worked, dancing in multiple clubs throughout the Midwest and I always tried to stay close. Kansas, Missouri, Iowa, Nebraska and South Dakota

I got home, pushed myself into "survival overdrive" and worked every night to quickly move out on my own.

were the extent of my travels. It was all so glamorous in the beginning and we did shows, choreographed dancing and stripping in "regular" bars and high end clubs. I never imagined this progression of lies and sin could take me to the places it did. I thought I had it all; a three bedroom house all finely furnished, all new everything, decorated perfect, I took meticulous care of everything, my home, my yard and flower garden, my outward appearance and I had a brand new red convertible in the driveway. I had at least one of everything and so did my daughter; I was in my early twenties. I did not talk to Blackie much and tore up most of his letters. I was angry on the inside. I was using men left and right and did not care much for any of them. I began to feel depressed. I remember going to work, thinking it was all glamorous and fun; it was a wild party every night. I was totally desensitized; I could do this job drinking or sober, no problem. There was so much money to be made. We would work the stage, the tables, or do what they called a "human sacrifice", the "Hot Seat", or a "body slam." Girls would pull the guys up on the stage and make a spectacle of him, especially for bachelor parties; whipped cream, confetti, autographing with sharpies, lipstick; all kinds of silliness for $50.00 to $100.00 for five minutes of fame in front of his friends! I've seen all kinds of craziness; from VIP rooms to standing showers that men could watch girls showering; completely disrespectful on both accounts.

Many things that I've witnessed are too disgraceful to write in this book, but eventually I began to feel a shift inside; I was noticing a lot of things becoming worse and more distasteful. However, at this point, I was like a money-making machine. I thought of myself as a business woman. I had my little black book, I knew which of my good tippers, regular customers were coming in to see me, at which clubs, on what nights, and I would pick and choose where to go each night to make the most money. Once I got there, I would not sit until I made my first $100 for the night. I would cash it in for a $100 bill and rubber-band it to my hip so that the customers knew I was serious and that if I walked over to their tables, I expected to make money; I wasn't stopping for single bills. I was arrogant and had an attitude and was in a lot of pain on the inside. This lifestyle had me sucked in, hook-line-and-sinker and the thought of getting out seemed impossible. It's a crazy, powerful feeling to be on a stage and have men laying down $100 bills and they can't touch you, take advantage, or do as they want with you. I felt protected in most of the clubs I worked in. The thought of leaving the ease of this was mind boggling but what it was taking from me and draining out of me was worse. I just was deceived at the time. It was just as addictive as a drug. I started to question, in my heart, how long I could keep this up. Things were starting to happen that made me question more and more. I did not feel good about some of the places I was working. Places I said I would never go. One night I was on my way to work with a friend that I worked with frequently and we were close. We both were really pretty "good girls" comparatively. We did not do drugs, drank some but not a lot, did <u>NOT</u> dance fully nude, and we had rules. Rules like: Never leave the bar with a customer, don't date customers, never accept a drink or food from customers, if the drink sat on the table, throw it out and get a new one! Don't give out personal information, walk to the car in pairs or groups, and <u>no prostitution!</u> These rules saved me from much harm, I am sure. My friend was a believer in God as I was; we would talk about it in the car a lot on the way to work. But we knew we were trapped by the circumstances and money and I was just living as if I could do what I wanted or needed to do and that I would be forgiven because God would understand. While I do believe whole heartedly in God's grace, I do not believe we can do as we please as a license to sin. I was in a dangerous, backslidden state and rarely went to church but for Easter. My focus and attention was not on God but thank God that His focus has always been on me! He doesn't give up on us!

As we were driving to work that evening, my friend Misty and I had the top down on my convertible and the music up loud. We were easy to spot; red convertible with the license plate HIMTNC (high maintenance abbreviated), our hair flying and us dancing around. A large car of African-American men cruised by us and spun their car around in the middle of traffic. Luckily, we were close to the strip club but I knew we were in trouble. I pulled over in front of the door as soon as I could and hopped in the backseat. The keys were still in the ignition; my car was a manual convertible, and I was pulling the top up as fast as I could. I locked it down and locked the doors and seconds after I did, my car was surrounded by those men. There were probably five to seven of them. I was trapped in the backseat and

Misty in the passenger seat; neither of us could drive off and we both felt paralyzed with fear. They began knocking on the windows and chanting profanity at us, asking if we were scared. Again, angels must have been dispatched! Not sure of what to do, I stayed still behind my friend's seat and told her don't worry or panic; to stay calm. I instructed her that if and when they moved toward the left of the car, I was going to flip the seat and she would flip the lock at the same time and I was pushing her out the door and we were going to make a sprint for the entrance to the club. I did not know if it would work, or if we would be fast enough but He did provide the door and at the time, that's all I could see. The plan did work and we were unharmed, shaken to the core and I was really beginning to

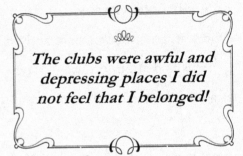

The clubs were awful and depressing places I did not feel that I belonged!

think about my life after this. I still did dangerous things though, depending on the dollar amount. Like taking a Greyhound bus all way to South Dakota to work for a week. The bus station is not a safe place in the middle of the night for young girls. The clubs were awful and depressing places I did not feel that I belonged!

In between work, I was driving, with my daughter, to the prison to see Blackie. I was afraid my daughter would not know him or remember him. I drove there often and when I would, the days were long to sit in the visiting area. To sit and talk and look at this whole situation was very difficult, to say the least. The only entertainment was the vending machines and event of picture taking for the family with a back drop of palm trees – palm trees!? As if we were to think we were in paradise, right!? Blackie began to say he was sorry and that he was leading a fellowship group in the prison and had rededicated his life to God and wanted his marriage to work. I wasn't hearing him and did not believe him. I wanted a divorce. At that time, it seemed difficult to get a divorce during incarceration. I made it clear that the reason I was there was for my daughter only and his relationship with her. No matter the circumstance, I believed that every girl (or person) had the right to know their father and I strongly believe in the father-daughter bond. The absence of that is tragic and detrimental. He would want me to stay the whole weekend if I made the drive so he gave me information of a ministry down the street from the prison called the "Agape House." It was for women and children of inmates. Looking back, I can't believe I did that but it may have saved our lives at the time. The house was safer than the rundown hotels around there. My daughter and I stayed there a few times and it was run by a little, old woman and her husband. They would fry chicken and make dinners and serve us; provide a family living area, and locks on each bedroom door to the halls and bathrooms. I hated this period in my life, but I was thankful for the ministry of this house. They only charged $7.00 a night.

Life did continue to get harder; the city wanted to shut certain clubs down. Cops started coming in regularly and in order to get places shut down, girls would get ticketed; labeled as "prostitution" if codes such as coverage, closeness to the customer less than so many inches away, and other things, weren't strictly adhered to. I had gone to Las Vegas and was partying with some friends when I received a phone call that the clubs had been raided and several girls were on this list; my name was one of them! I could not believe it! I had been ticketed a couple of times and had been ticketed for being a minor and drinking in the club under twenty years of age, but this?! This set my anxiety off; I was so nervous that I was in the bathroom throwing up for a long time! I had a mindset, as many strippers do, that "I am a dancer, not a prostitute!" I thought what I was doing was somehow better, more acceptable and less degrading, glamorous, of course!! What a deception!! I think sin can take us anywhere if we allow it to get a foothold. I know I've made many decisions I regret.

Around Christmas time, I found myself pregnant; the father did not want anything to do with this situation. He did not love me or want me and definitely did not want a baby! I called his house and he hung up the phone on me. I searched for Karen; she was now separated from her husband and I knew that she had had an abortion before. She did try to make me think about it, but at the same time she supported my decision and took me for the procedure. I was upset, but again, that lie had resurfaced that it would be another child in the world like me – unwanted and abandoned – not worthy and "fatherless", I could not stand it! I could not allow a repeat of me! That is what I thought. My desire for the whole lifestyle was dwindling; I was empty. I had to get attorneys to get rid of these ridiculous tickets and clear my name. I remember that I got to the point that as soon as I walked in the club, I would hand the emcee $65.00 or $70.00 to skip my name on the call list for the stage rotation. The stage with the mirrors that I once loved, now for some reason I could not stand to be in front of them. I did not want to see myself this way anymore.

As I was on the endless search for new clubs and fresh places to make more money I ran into an old childhood friend named Stacey. Stacey and her friend Anny were now working at a massage parlor in Kansas City. Stacey was going on and on about this "easy" money. She really never felt that she had the body to dance but she was a very pretty girl. She now was in a bi-sexual relationship with her best friend Anny. They were also into witchcraft. They loved working at the massage parlor. I had gone back and shared with my friend, Karen about this "fast, easy money maker". I asked Karen if she had ever heard of a place like this. She was instantly interested and wanted to go check it out with me. A few days later Karen and I drove down to "The Boulevard" in Kansas City. There it sat, a small parlor on the edge of the Boulevard, with maroon awnings and appeared to look professional on the outside. As we walked through the door, the second entrance was locked. The lady sitting at the front desk opened up a little glass window, said "hello" and buzzed us in. Once inside Karen and I introduced ourselves and I let them know that I was a friend of Stacey's. A few minutes later, Mrs. B entered the room. She was not a very attractive lady. She had dirty blonde hair with an out of style hairdo, thick glasses and make-up that appeared like the 1970's. I remember her wearing a knee-length, off-white skirt with coffee colored pantyhose and low heeled off white shoes. She reminded me of a lady who worked at K-Mart in the 80's! She seemed to have a "fake friendly" attitude and character. I remember her telling us that before we could actually start making money, we would have to do a few days of studying "The Massage Menu", as she handed us the menu book with a full description of each massage type and pricing. We also would need to spend the first week folding and doing all of the laundry and towels for the parlor, to make sure each room was fresh and ready to go. After that all the girls would rotate doing the laundry for rooms they had serviced. That seemed easy enough so Karen and I began doing laundry and studying the "Parlor Menu". I was also instructed that this was a professional place of business and that there were no "happy ending" massages given there and anyone caught doing this would be immediately fired. This was a place where "professional men" came to relax. Men like doctors, lawyers, pro-athletes, and wealthy businessmen. The next day later, Mrs. B gave me the grand tour of the parlor. As I walked down the corridor, room after room and glancing, it seemed each room featured the same type furnishings with a little different theme. There were grand large Jacuzzi bathtubs "for two", mirrors all over the walls, places for champagne bottles to be kept on ice and low lying massage beds. As I looked around, I spotted in the corner of each room what looked like a camera. She would keep an eye out and monitored things to make sure everyone was safe and not breaking any rules. Just walking through those rooms that day gave me a sick feeling in my stomach and a very uneasy and edgy feeling. I think she sensed that from me. Next, she took me into a break room type area. There she appealed to my senses and awakened my curiosity once again. She brought me into a room where all over the wall hung photographs of many different women in beautiful modeling portraits, glamour photography, and pretty, sexy poses of them with their "fake names" next to each portrait. She said, "Your picture will be hung on this wall and each client (man) will get to enter this room first and choose which lady he would like to hire for massage. It was all painted up a pretty, professional, safe, and upscale picture. The money to be made was very alluring and enticing. Thoughts were running wild in my mind. I knew something was just not right. Every time I envisioned myself being totally alone with a man, a stranger, in one of those rooms, behind a locked door, my heart would race! What could be "safe" about this? These thoughts of protection had to be coming from somewhere? Just then I returned back downstairs to Karen who was still doing laundry. A few moments later, I could sense that the other girls coming in and out were not too happy about us being there. Jealousies and competitive spirits were already moving into high gear. Then to my dismay and wrenching disgust, two red-headed women walked in toward us and were talking to each other and in that moment I discovered that they were a "mother and daughter" team working there together! Something in my spirit cried, "NO"!! See, even when we make poor decisions and get off track, going our own way, if we have known God—He never leaves us! He is big enough to keep us! It is up to us to listen and hear. Just then I heard that "still small voice" saying to me, "Get out of here! You do not belong here; this is not for you…Do Not Return"! Karen and I left; I explained to her that I would not be coming back to that place. This was clearly not for me! Praise God, we never worked a day in that place! Laundry service and the grand tour was more than enough for me. God rarely screams, so if we are quiet enough to listen, we can hear Him, even when we are doing wrong. God is Love. He will lead us in our correct path, but we must desire it and obey. In my final analysis of "the parlor on the boulevard", there was much prostitution going on in that place! It was definitely a place of deceit and wickedness. It was an illusion of glamour.

Again, in my search for love and attention, I accepted a date with the Devil!

In the early 90's as my life was SURELY spiraling out of control. I could see God's hand was CLEARLY on my life. Just before I finally threw in the towel on my old life, I faced a situation that could've changed my life forever. Again, in my search for love and attention, I accepted a date with the Devil! I was dancing at a high-end club in Kansas. Professional athletes, celebrities and well known people did frequent this club often. One night, in walked a famous man; he was the buzz of Kansas City at the time. He was an athlete and was filming a movie during that time period. He would not stay away from me; he was captured by me on the stage and requesting my phone number and a date. Curiosity won over and intrigue got the best of me. We went out dancing at the most popular club at the time and people were all around him, girls hovering, and people requesting autographs. Being with him was a strange, exciting, and alluring feeling. On one of our dates I had been drinking heavily. I was drunk. We left the bar and drove for miles, a very long time. When we arrived at his home I had no idea where we were, just that it was far away from home. I quickly realized there were things in his house that I wanted no part of. It was apparent that he had a very wild side and very liberal with sex. We were still having fun at this point and kissing and things were heating up. Things began happening that shouldn't have and I remember him pinning me to the carpet in his front room floor being very demanding. Instantly I became sober, once again hearing that still small voice, "Get away from him, don't be with him, and get out of here". I began trying to push him away from me, trying to be nice and told him I could not be with him without using protection and made excuses. He got up, began throwing things across the room, being forceful toward me and he was very angry. His whole demeanor had changed. I grabbed my purse and ran out of the door of his condo the first chance I saw. He chased after me. It was cold outside and I was demanding a taxi to get me home and if not I was going to scream and go to the neighbors and make a scene. I did get a taxi ride. I had a very terrible feeling about that night and about him in general. Approximately a year later it aired on television that this man had been confirmed as HIV positive. In later years, he passed away with symptoms of AIDS. My

Jesus has surely protected, guarded, preserved, and spared my life. I give all my gratitude to Him alone! If I hadn't escaped this situation when I did, mere moments could've changed my life forever and or ended it. God spared me from <u>ever</u> having any type of disease!

Everything just kept getting worse; my daughter was close to four years old and Blackie was about to be released to a halfway house in Kansas City. I hadn't seen him in six months; they had shipped him in the middle of the night to North Dakota. We made that trip just before Christmas once and he had tried hard to convince me that he was changed and we should stay married. I really did not want to stay married, I just wanted a divorce. Then, to top it all off, for the second Christmas in a row, I found myself pregnant, again! This time I was very emotionally attached to the father and it was hard; I was in a very bad situation now. It was winter and I was broke. He completely blew me off and I tried to call his parents, but they just hung up on me. When your occupation is a dancer, people in the "real world" don't have much respect for you and treat you as beneath them. I was more lost than ever! I was scheduled to go to work in Iowa for the week. I needed money to pay for my situation. I did not feel good, I was depressed, and I did not want to dance but I had no choice. I knew this club was getting "harder," several of the girls were turning to prostitution and flying to New York for their "boyfriends" who were really pimps. The dancing had progressed to another level. As sin always does, it leads to death! It was an awful week; I was nauseous, tired and feeling sick of my job. The girls decided they hated me and began making a plan to jump me in the dressing room and beat me up. They were mad because one of their "boyfriend pimps" had come in the club and wouldn't stay away from the stage when I was on it. He wanted to talk to me at his table and he was complimenting me non-stop. Looking back now, I am glad those girls intervened and stopped me from talking to him. The enemy has a way of painting pretty pictures of lies and deception and entrapment. My friend, who was with me, explained my situation to the girls and pleaded on my behalf. After all, I did not approach that guy at all; I just wanted to go home. It seemed like one thing after another kept happening. One girl was in the dressing room on the pay phone every night calling her psychic for help and answers and the final cherry on the top was this: I was in the dressing room when a girl I'd never seen before came in and undressed; she had had a breast surgery for sure but I turned around and that was no girl!! I was ready to leave asap! I got home, went for my procedure and when I was there, the nurse gave me an Ativan or Valium. I remember I tried to call Tony in hopes he would say, "I love you Dana, don't do it!" but that wasn't the case, a girl answered his phone and was laughing with him, I just hung up. This time I had problems medically and my blood pressure was fluctuating; I had to stay longer. I went right back to work, determined to be done with stupid decisions and men for a while!

One of my latter memories of dancing was at a club in Kansas. Karen and her boyfriend came to see me and I got so drunk that I could hear

127

the whisper of the enemy, "Go ahead, and compete with those girls out there going nude!" I was heavily thinking about it. Would that bring a new high and revive me – would I make more money? Thank God somehow that thought was cast out. However, I did get so drunk that night that I did not remember much of my last set and I passed out, undressed, on the dirty floor of the dressing room. Karen came back to the room and a couple of my friends dressed me in my jeans and they literally carried me out of that club! I remember getting violently sick in the backseat and out of the car window down the highway. When I got to my house, I could not get the key in the door. My mom let me in, she was babysitting. The next morning was the absolute worst and a definite turning point for me. When I woke up in the morning my mom was gone, she had to go to work. For the first time ever, I woke up still drunk. I was walking into walls. I tried to take a bath to wake up but nothing was helping! Did they put something in my drinks? All I knew was that it was morning and I was not sober and this was not acceptable. My daughter was about to wake up! This was against my rules, my plan, and my vow. I was very angry. We napped and relaxed, watching cartoons most of that morning. This caused me to dig through the phone book for colleges. Today, we visit this same strip club monthly and give gifts in the same dressing room that I once laid on the floor, lost and believing lies. The gifts contain what I needed to hear that day; TRUTH and LOVE! I found the nearest beauty college, called them immediately and enrolled that day! I wanted a way out. I gave it all I had. I needed around 1,600 hours. I went for months and got to 886 hours. It was more than halfway done and I gave up. I was in school forty hours a week. I applied for housing and food stamps and daycare assistance. I was dancing at night for extra money but I could not keep up the pace any longer. I was exhausted! I could not see a way out, completely out! Blackie was being released from prison and my patience was thin. The "life" had a hold of me in many ways. For me, the seduction was power; power over men, my own life, controlling my own decision and finances. It was power to know that I could do all this and have all that I had and do it by myself. How could I really do this cutting hair or any other job without higher education involved? How could I go

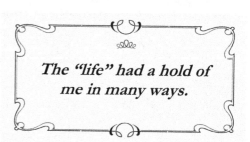

The "life" had a hold of me in many ways.

to school full time and survive with all the things I now had to pay for and keep up? Although dancing seemed to solve some problems for me and what I thought was the solution to my problems, it also was taking from me and I did not even know it. Closing in on some of the latter days of dancing, a couple of situations occurred that really caused me to step back and think about the life that I was living...

The first one happened as we were on our way to work one night. Some girls and I were in the car, it was early evening and we decided to stop at an adult store that sold costumes, lingerie, and high heels. We had been there in the past to purchase outfits before work. This store was in a very bad part of the city, a very dangerous area at night. On this particular night a girl came out from behind a door and she introduced herself to us. She was tall and skinny, with stringy, blonde hair. She appeared disheveled and weary. She had dark circles under her eyes. She smiled and said "My name is Katie." We'd never seen her before so we inquired about her job; was she a cashier there? She began explaining to us that she did "shows" there. My attention was caught. I asked what kind of "shows" and she offered to show me the "show rooms." I hesitantly walked through a small corridor and she pushed the door wide open. It was a tiny "booth" room with one chair, a box of Kleenex and see through glass wall in front of it. On the inside of the glass was a padded type area where a girl would lay. I felt sick and probably gasped. I quickly turned to her and compassionately asked "Why would you do this?!?" I was questioning "How much do you make? I instinctively fell into rescue mode! I said "You don't have to do this! Why don't you dance?? You could work dancing with us for one night and make more than all week doing this!" She said she was comfortable there, but would think about it.

A week or so passed and I thought about her from time to time. Looking back now I can see even then I wanted to help to "empower" women. Then I got a phone call from a dancer, cancelling for the night and we were short a person. My mind went to Katie at the store. We called her and stopped by to pick her up to come work with us for the night. Even though I wanted to help her, I knew it wasn't a good decision once we were on the road. We were headed to Leavenworth, Kansas. I knew the manager was very picky and selective and he probably wasn't going to be very happy with my decision. She wasn't very attractive, had bad teeth and I just plain felt sorry for her! We all talked to her on the way to the club and she began to tell us about a customer who would bring in a diaper, pay her to urinate on it in front of him and then take it home with him! I could barely drive the car! I wanted to throw up and my heart raged with anger toward men. Hearing that just confirmed to me how sick people are! We are all LOST and SIN SICK without a Savior! I hoped that things would change for her. She said she had to do anything to make money, she had five kids at home and her boyfriend did not work. He stayed home with them, and he sent her to work in the adult store. In all those years, that was one of the most disgusting things anyone in the industry had ever shared with me!

We are all LOST and SIN SICK without a Savior!

The next night after work, the girls and I decided to stop by that same store knowing that there was a "juice bar" in the back, up the stairs. Just out of curiosity we went up to check it out and see if it was that bad of a place to work or not. We spiraled up the long winding staircase, up the back of the old, rickety building, and as we walked through the door at the top of the last step, we entered a very small, smoke-filled atmosphere. I glanced to my left and, to my horror; there stood a very young, African-American girl largely pregnant and fully nude. She appeared barefoot and ready to burst at any moment.

The girl looked too miserable to dance! She was just waddling around, from man to man, for dollar bills. I was appalled! I am sure tears were welled up in my eyes, if not streaming down my face. She seemed desperate and lost! We quickly left the bar, stirred with emotion, and my mind began to race with thoughts about quitting my job! I had seen a terrible progression over the last few days and I certainly would never want to be in that position! It took a long time to get the images of those two situations put to rest. What was I going to do to begin to implement change? I needed to see light at the end of the tunnel! I needed to "wake up!!" My eyes were beginning to open, I wanted to get out but I was so reliant on the money and I had to financially support us. I wasn't going to go down broke. When I looked at my daughter, I always thought about the best for her and her future and then a light bulb came on. She was four years old and it hit me that one day she might catch on to what I was doing, my real "modeling job," and then fright set in. What if she grew up and chose to do what was role modeled before her? What if "the life" was her example? These thoughts set off a reign of terror! Then I got the call that Blackie was released in Kansas City; he needed to be picked up at the Kansas City bus station. It was late at night, so his friend drove us to pick him up. I saw him face-to-face, after four years, free. I was happy for him but I wasn't happy for me. I had a lot of decisions to make. He did not look like the man I knew – changed on the outside but what about the inside? We dropped him off at the halfway house. My daughter remembered him and loved him and I was glad for that.

Soon after, I knew it would never work out for us again. I did not let him move in our house, our safe place. I tested his behavior. We just could not get along. He cheated with a girl I worked with right away and I wouldn't commit to him either. It was too complicated and there was too much water under the bridge. He was trying to pursue me and date someone else. When I finally said no, he got angry and threw a brush across the room at my head and that was the end; the first sign of violence again. I called 911 and asked him to leave. In the future years, I can say it was never easy but he had a strong relationship with my daughter; he loved her and he always remained faithful in paying his child support. Today he is remarried and to my knowledge he is serving the Lord in a local church! He recently shared with me that he is preaching in prisons and doing prison ministry!! Amen! I was thankful for these things; but I began to feel more depressed and desperate in my lifestyle.

At this point, I did a very foolish thing. My friend had been telling me that she had been visiting a psychic for help with her future and decisions. I knew better than this but I was enticed, I needed answers; I needed help. I called her and set up an appointment. It was close to my house surprisingly. She asked me to bring a cassette tape so I could have the session to replay. I went to her house and I was shocked. The house was in upper-middle class suburbia; home interiors on the walls, dad making cookies and kids getting off the school bus at her house. I went in and she was sitting at a dining table with regular cards. The devil is such a liar and a deceiver; all appeared so normal. The first words out of my mouth were "Hi, before we get started I just have to know if you believe in Jesus Christ?" She said "Yes" and I told her that I was not there because I was not a believer or against God, but just wanted to see if she had some insight or answers for me. I told her I did not want her to tell me or say anything regarding my family, etc., just about me. I knew being there was wrong, but I was simply burnt out and desperate! She recorded the conversation. The things she said were not 100% accurate. God's word is the only thing that is 100% accurate! I left there with my tape. I went home and was more depressed than ever and could not figure out what was wrong with me! I remember lying on my brand new, blue sofa. One of my good customers had given me a tip; $1,800.00, and I had used it to buy new furniture. I looked around my house, there was nothing I lacked, yet something was missing. I felt like I just had a piece of my life that was empty. I had no real security. My daughter and I were fine financially, but there was this draining, nagging, emptiness.

At this same time my mother, of all people, began calling me and bothering me about visiting this church that she had been going to. She was the very last person that I wanted to hear from about church. I had been allowing her to take my daughter to church, wasn't that enough? She began telling me how she had gotten "saved" and how much she loved this church and the pastor there. She told me that she was saving and gathering money to sign up to go on a trip with the church. She was planning to go to Israel, the Holy Land, and that she was going to be baptized in the Jordan River by the pastor of her new church! I really did not want to hear her or visit the church. I was busy trying to figure out how I was going to solve my problems and what my next steps were going to be. Was I going to file for divorce? Switch clubs where I was working to feel safer and hopefully not get in anymore trouble? Or schedule more out of town jobs? I started working at a new club in Kansas City but for some reason I just could not stand to be on the stage there either! What in the world was going on with me? I now believe someone was praying and interceding for me! This club was tightly controlled, I knew the owner very well and I felt safe. However, at this particular club

I now believe someone was praying and interceding for me!

there were many very powerful men that frequented it nightly. Over the years, I had known a lot of people. from professional athletes, celebrities, musicians, rock stars, doctors, lawyers, wealthy businessmen; to men and families connected with organized crime. This club was relatively safe for me but on the inside it had a different climate of customers and activity. As I said, the men were very powerful and that's all I am going to say about that. I did not work there for long but each night when I went to work, select men would come to see me, order bottles of champagne in the VIP area lay down several $100 bills and want me to sit at their table all night. I was making a lot of money, paying to skip my stage rotation and a new level of fear had set in. These were not the type of men to get involved with or to upset in any way. In the meantime, my mother was hounding me about church. By this time my mother had completely given up alcohol and cigarettes; her life had changed. To this day, she hasn't had a drop of alcohol or a cigarette in over twenty years and that is an amazing deliverance! I saw this so I finally caved in to her request.

Photo Gallery

Images of One Life

Divinely Rescued & Powerfully Transformed

Dana approximately 5 years old

My powder blue dress and white ribbon, worn to my grandma's (Mom's) funeral

Dana 8 years old, at Janis's wedding in the Holly Hobby dress 1978 (the year of the sexual abuse)

Dana~7th grade 13 years old, on the road to rebellion-hanging out at a neighborhood motorcycle shop

Dana~ Miss Budweiser 1989 at Diamond Joe's Gentleman's Club

Dana~19 and pregnant awaiting Blackie's sentencing

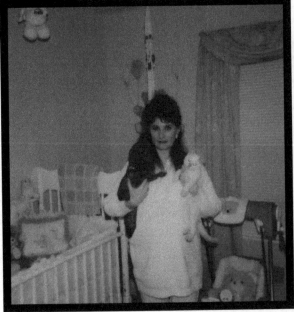

Dana with oldest daughter
(single momma 1991)

Dana (Brittany) & Elite
Ladies ShowGirls Poster
for Shows at Clubs

Sheffield Family Life Center Kansas City, MO - January 1994 Where I got saved and surrendered it All

My Mother being baptized in the Jordan River in Israel with Dr. George Westlake Pastor Emeritus at Sheffield Family Life Center

My Mother at the Wailing Wall, Jerusalem~ Israel Trip with Dr. George Westlake Pastor Emeritus & SFLC Church

Rocky & Dana's Wedding Bahamas 2000

Rocky & Dana On Our Honeymoon Bahamas 2000

Dana & youngest daughter approximately 2001 at church

*Dana's College Graduation
with Daughters
Associate of Arts Degree
2002*

*Dana's Nursing
Graduation
Bachelor of Science Degree,
RN 2005*

Our 10 Year anniversary
Bahamas 2010

Rocky & Dana with Pastor Miles McPherson,
The Rock Church San Diego

Dana with Heather & JC's Girls Las Vegas Outreach 2011 Preparing for ministry in Kansas City

Dana McCartney Candillo, Founder, The Lion's Beauty Queens, Inc. August 2011

LBQ Kansas City 1st <u>Official Full Outreach</u> Oct 2011

Dana 1st meeting Lisa Bevere, great woman of faith- my inspiration, at GodChicks Conference 2012 Hollywood, CA

Lisa Bevere &
Dana at
GodChicks
Conference
2012
Hollywood, CA

Lisa Bevere with
Dana & LBQ at
GodChicks
Leadership
Breakfast 2012

Original Lion's Beauty Queens making our way to Cali (Elena, Dana, Starla) Doors opening for ministry in Oceanside and San Diego, CA

Dana with Pastor Leanne Matthesius at C3 Church, My Church in San Diego, California 2014

Our Family Christmas 2012

20 years later, Dana with Dr. George Westlake Pastor Emeritus at Sheffield Family Life Center Saved by Grace under his ministry January 1994

Dana McCartney Candillo

Dana's house on Park Street Abandoned and Condemned

Dana's house on Park Street being Restored
He makes ALL things NEW

"The House That Built Me" by *Miranda Lambert*

I know they say you can't go home again

I just had to come back one last time

Ma'am, I know you don't know me from Adam

But these hand prints on the front steps are mine

Up those stairs in that little back bedroom

Is where I did my homework and I learned to play guitar

And I bet you did not know under that live oak

My favorite dog is buried in the yard

I thought if I could touch this place or feel it

This brokenness inside me might start healing

Out here it's like I am someone else

I thought that maybe I could find myself

If I could just come in, I swear I'll leave

Won't take nothing but a memory

From the house that built me

You leave home, you move on

And you do the best you can

I got lost in this whole world

And forgot who I am

The Third Trimester

"And they overcame [their accuser] by the blood of the lamb and by the word of their testimony..."
~Revelation 12:11 NKVJ

"...Even if I bear witness of Myself, My witness is true, for I know where I came from and where I am going..."
~John 8:14 NKJV

"Time After Time" by *Cyndi Lauper*
(My conversations with God)

Lyin' in my bed I hear the clock tick
And think of you
Caught up in circles confusion
Is nothing new
Flashback warm nights
Almost left behind
Suitcase of memories
Time after time

Sometimes you picture me
I am walking too far ahead
You're calling to me I can't hear
What you've said
Then you say go slow
I fall behind
The second hand unwinds

If you're lost you can look and you will find me
Time after time
If you fall I will catch you I'll be waiting
Time after time

After my picture fades and darkness
Has turned to gray
Watching through windows
You're wondering if I am okay
Secrets stolen from deep inside
The drum beats out of time

Chapter 3 Overcomer
Salvation, 1994 & Current Marriage

In January of 1994, I had just turned twenty four years old when I walked through the doors of Sheffield Family Life Center in Northeast Kansas City for the first time. I had on white jeans, a colorful shirt, big hair, make-up, long red fingernails and my red stilettos. I hadn't really been to church in years unless it was on Easter or Christmas service somewhere and that would've been rare. The praise and worship music was loud and intense. I remember looking around and there were people with their hands lifted high and tears were flowing. I remember men with their hands raised. This really caught my attention. Something dropped in my spirit, "that is what a real man is!!" I was impressed watching the men of the church and their reverence toward the Lord. There was POWER in that place! A presence – the room was filled with the Holy Spirit! I felt like I had ocean waves in my stomach, rushing and rushing; it was electric. I felt something I'd never felt before. Then, the most awesome man of God entered the platform – Dr. George Westlake, Jr. – and he was praising God over and over, as if scripture in the book of Revelation was being poured out. Holy, Holy, Holy!!! There was something intriguing to me about his voice; he was on fire for God!! It was as if I could hear the Lord through him. He preached like no one I'd ever heard, with authority and confidence. He seemed genuine and desperate at his attempt to see people move and come forward to accept Jesus Christ as Lord and Savior. When he spoke, it felt like the message was speaking directly to me and my situation. He seemed to really care and relate to the congregation. My heart was touched and I am sure I had tears streaming; I wanted to go forward. Just then I heard this whisper in my mind (the devil is a liar and deceiver) that I could not go down to the altar. I had been too bad, I had to go to work, I had bills to pay and I could not quit my job yet! I did not have money or a plan for that!! So I turned my back and as service ended, I walked out the door. I thought a lot about it over the week; I never doubted who God was and I had never felt that kind of authentic, powerful presence and sensed Him in that magnitude. That week I still felt depressed, still faced all the same problems and still thought about getting out of the industry. I just could not see any way possible. But God is the God of the impossible! A Way maker! The next week I went back to Sheffield on Sunday morning and Pastor George Westlake was there preaching again. I could not wait until he called for the altar call. The same experience I felt the week prior was happening again. I raced to the altar and gave my life, surrendered it ALL, to Jesus Christ. I felt like bricks were lifted and it was ALL OVER! I knew that day that I was changed and that I was going to be changed more; a transformation had begun in me; the transformation from "Stripper to Saint!" I find it amazing that God used a mighty vessel of His, named "George," to plant the seed of TRUTH and bring me out of the darkness and into His light. In prior years, the enemy used a vessel named "George," his counterfeit, to instill lies, fears, anxieties, insecurities and abuse in many forms in the hopes of killing, stealing and destroying me. In the garden, Jesus crushed the head of the serpent; he is the father of lies. The Word of God is TRIUMPHANT and in Him we have victory and authority! He reigns in the heavens therefore we reign on earth! The eyes of my head and heart were now fully open!

I remember the next day, sitting in my living room, looking around, wondering what I was going to do next. One of my friends, who also was a dancer, had been staying with me. She was there that morning. She was very pregnant and getting ready to give her baby up for adoption. I told her "I think we need to find a job today!" She kind of laughed at me and said "Okay." I remember thinking "I guess I will try praying – I haven't done that in a while." I went and got the big book of yellow pages and wondered where I could apply for a job that my ego could handle. I did not want to wait tables or work fast food. I opened the phonebook to fitness centers. Gold's Gym to be exact. I figured that might be fun and attractive people probably worked there, I possibly could fit in there. I had no experience but I got all ready and dressed and Anna and I went to the gym and quickly filled out a "real" job application. Next, a man walked out from behind the counter and introduced himself. He was older and good looking. I guessed he must have been the boss. He asked me to come into his office; he wanted to interview me on the spot. He was looking at me intently and asked me a lot of questions. He was somewhat sarcastic and joked saying I seemed very spoiled – what had I been doing for a living? How was I so young and had a new convertible, cell phone, home, hair, nails, clothing, etc. I did not tell him about my seven year career; I could tell he was interested in me. I sensed that he was flirting with me. I asked him if he was the owner or the manager. He said he was the owner. I was somewhat curious about him. I left and he called one of his managers, who was also his best friend, and told him he thought his future wife just walked through the door and that I was the most beautiful woman he'd ever seen. His name was Shawn; he called me immediately following that interview. He said he would hire me but he would rather go out with me. He wanted to know if I would go on a date with him. I said, okay, he had my interest. I could tell he was a powerful man, good-looking, wealthy and he was offering me a job. He showed up at my house to get to know me better and to talk about a date he wanted to take me on and a company party. He pulled up in a white corvette. He came in, we hung out and talked for quite awhile and he did kiss me. However, to my dismay, that was it. He told me that he was a Christian. I thought "WOW God, you work fast!!" He did not try to do anything inappropriate and said that he was waiting for marriage to have sex again because he had made so many past mistakes. He'd never been married, no children and was quite a bit older than me. He was different than the men I had been dating. He gave me a job for $6.00 an hour. I was thankful but it was awful! I wasn't used to this; it was hard. I could not keep up with my house and bills because I was no longer stripping. Looking back, I think I served more as a "project" for Shawn. He wanted to rescue me but unfortunately it felt like he wanted to parent me. We were more like good friends than boyfriend and girlfriend. However, I am convinced that God did place him in my life for a reason.

During this time, as I was working for him full time, I was about to lose my house because I could not keep up making just $6.00 an hour. Shawn made an offer for my daughter and I to come stay with him. He had an extra bedroom. I went from full time to part time and still paid my car payment and bills. He made me be responsible. I cooked and cleaned for him but the most important thing was that God used this time for me to get "alone" with HIM! The TV was rarely ever on any other channel than the Christian networks, I read the Bible, checked out every movie and stories about Jesus' life and biblical accounts. I learned a lot. I was going to Sheffield Family Life Center Sunday morning, Sunday night and Wednesday night and taking my daughter. We went alone. Shawn did not feel the need to go to church to be saved, he just stayed home and watched Christian television. I needed more than that. I needed to be in God's powerful presence. I could sense Him changing and transforming me. Every time Pastor Westlake spoke, I was like a sponge; soaking it all in! It was as if time stood still and nothing else mattered but the truth, knowledge, and revelation that were entering my mind, heart and life. I became more and more focused on the Lord and the changes that were happening in me to become a Christ follower, a better person, and Christian mother. I wanted to set a good example for my daughter and teach her about God. This was a very peaceful period in my life in which a lot of learning, molding and shaping took place. However, I was a very young woman still, twenty four years old, and I did desire a husband and to have a "real family" life. I wanted the white picket fence, the fairytale that all girls dreamed of having. I wanted more children. Shawn assured me that he wanted this too but as time continued to pass, we continued to just be "roommates." Friendship and living together grew frustrating for me and just did not seem like the thing I should be doing anymore. Broken promises and lack of fulfillment set in and I decided that I needed to move out and try to move on but one problem persisted; finances. I had never been out on my own and not danced for a living. I got a small job at a retail store, filed for Section Eight Housing and food stamps went to food pantries and vowed to never look back at my old lifestyle. It was hard, but I can say, strangely, I never felt tempted. I knew my heart was different, changed, not perfect, but saved and set free! I still fell down and made mistakes but got back up – I was now living under grace! Still, financially it was not fun.

Still back and forth with Shawn, as his last attempt to make the relationship work he popped the question. Plans for a honeymoon in Hawaii were made as he purchased a 17k diamond. Next he said I could quit my $6.00 an hour job at the gym in which I worked for him. Then he proceeded to purchase me a brand new car, a beautiful pearl-white Riviera. Prior to the brief engagement, he bought a 6300 sq. ft. home on five acres to ensure that it would not be considered "marital property". I found out later any documents that I had signed regarding the house and property were meaningless. The wedding was planned in two weeks and I was whisked away to Hawaii. I was feeling excited, rushed, and nervous. I remember gazing out my balcony at an infinite blue line; I had never seen the ocean before. I walked down from my hotel room; slipped out of my flip flops and my feet felt the soft, warm sand for the first time. Taking it all in, I walked slowly, the sand crushing softly between my toes to the edge of the new blue world. I sat down in the sand; I was in awe of the magnificent beauty of this ocean filled with so many vibrant hues. It was like a heavenly dream for me. I was instantly mesmerized and drawn to the loveliness of God's creation. Today it is still my favorite place to be. The patterns of the unstoppable, never ceasing waves prove God's existence; power, strength, and stunning majesty. In this setting is where I feel, see, and hear God the most. In 1995 I fell in love with this wonder of the earth. Surely, this small town girl had never come in contact with anything quite comparable in Independence, Missouri! However, as I took in all the beauty of Maui and Kauai I still did not feel complete in my marriage vow. It lacked true intimacy. As I returned home I felt very secure but surrounded by control and walls that were closing in on me. The house was beautiful and decorated to perfection but my days were lonely. When Shawn was home from his vigorous business, it seemed like we were roommates at best. I was thankful for all that I had, but I felt like a trapped bird. I questioned my decision about the marriage from day one. As I had prepared the wedding invitations, the front of them were designed with a

Cinderella castle and a bride and groom on a horse headed toward that beautiful place. Surely, now in this castle I was just alone like a solitary bird in a perfect golden cage. I had no idea of anything that was really going on within the marriage. Checks were written to the grocery store for me with his signature. He accounted for every dime. Any thing I did was rationed to me and I had no control over any decision. I knew that this union did not portray 1 Corinthians 13, "The way of Love". He was a good man, but the marriage still felt like more of a friendship and he was very dominating. I got pregnant on the honeymoon and soon had a miscarriage. I quickly doubted my decision. The marriage just lacked passion and chemistry and felt more like a contract and a good friendship. I was not content or satisfied. A few years down the road, in October, I did have one very beautiful daughter from this marriage. My daughters are the loves of my life. Having my babies was the greatest joy and the highlight of my entire life. I love them both so much!

Soon I found myself alone, single-parenting two girls and praying for wisdom and my future. One thing in mind for sure was that earthly castles and kings would not again fool me. I believed that God would provide for me and if I was to be married, I would need to make that decision based on Godly wisdom and God's Word. As far as a horse and rider…I know for me He will come in the end. Revelation 19:11-16 (MSG) says, "Then I saw Heaven open wide – and oh! A white horse and its rider. The Rider, named Faithful and True…On his robe and thigh is written, King of King, Lord of Lords."

Although divorce is a very ugly and undesirable thing, it happened to me again for the second time. I will always regret causing pain through this; I acknowledge that and can only ask for forgiveness. I remained going to church alone, with my daughters and we divorced. It was a very hard, difficult process and very frustrating. For all involved, it was an all out courtroom war for two and a half years. Out of respect for my youngest daughter, I'll leave it at that. To this day, we remain cordial friends and continue to co-parent to the best of our abilities; let the past be the past and raise her up to be a successful, Godly girl!

In the midst of all this, I had grown a lot and learned a lot. I went to church all the time. But an important note is that "church" did not save me. The personal relationship that I had opened up to and developed with the Savior, Jesus Christ is what saved me, graced me, and ultimately transformed my heart, mind and soul. I cannot say that I know the Bible front to back, but I can testify to a radical and extreme conversion that I would compare to be very similar to a "Paul, the Apostle" conversion on the Damascus Road. His glory has been revealed to me and His presence powerfully known. He has shown Himself real to me time after time. During this first year and a half that I was attending church at Sheffield I was inviting a lot of people to come to church with me. I had this burning feeling to call girls that I knew who were dancing and invite them. I had found truth and this wonderful, loving presence in God. I wanted others to experience what I was experiencing and feeling. I felt like I had introduced a lot of girls to that old lifestyle and I felt compelled to go back, share the truth and let them know there is freedom in Christ! I was constantly burning up the phone lines weekly to girls I'd left behind, inviting them to come to church with me. Several came, many out of curiosity about the changes in me.

No One believed that I would never go back to "the life." But I was very serious and determined to overcome! I had a vision set in my heart at this time. That was 1994. I constantly thought about how I could return to the strip clubs and talk to girls. My mind spun with thoughts: "How could I do this?" "Would they listen?" I would never want to offend or do harm. How would I go about this? I thought a great idea would be to go in, sit at a table and give a tip – only not for a dance but just to talk. Then I had thoughts about setting up a table in the dressing room and giving out information! I thought these were good ideas but how, who, and why would a manager ever let me in the door to do this?! I thought about sending flowers with notes – but that was no contact…I felt frustrated with the ideas and it seemed hopeless. It certainly wasn't making sense at that time and I felt like I needed a couple of girls to partner with and go with me. I knew no one who would be willing to do this and I knew no one who was experiencing this kind of conversion.

During the time of my divorce, I was living back at my mother's with my daughters. It was now 1999; those thoughts that I had put on the back burner were re-surfacing. I called my uncle, who was a pastor, and shared with him about my vision. At that time he told me that he felt that I hadn't been saved long enough. I needed to get really grounded and he was concerned about how the church would receive a ministry like this!? This added to my frustration, but I can see now that there was probably some wisdom in that advice. However, the thoughts persisted. I remember going to church and walking along the front side walk in front of Sheffield and pondering thoughts, "What if I just went to the pastor and shared my story and vision about a ministry in Kansas City?" Then I would get flooded with feelings of fear and shame and was just too afraid to

> *I would get flooded with feelings of fear and shame and was just too afraid to reveal that truth about my personal life.*

reveal that truth about my personal life. Thank God His truth is greater than my truth! I decided once again to place these thoughts and ideas on the back burner. The timing just did not seem right. I did not really know many people at this large church but I always felt comfortable and accepted there. I loved being there! I loved listening to Pastor Westlake, it seemed like every message that he delivered, spoke directly to me. I was hearing the truth with clarity!

In the midst of this time frame, I went to church one Sunday with a friend. As we were leaving the morning service, we were outside on the front sidewalk and a man was standing there. My friend immediately said, "Hi Pastor Rocky! How are you doing!?" She shook his hand. He turned to me, shook my hand and introduced himself to me. I learned he was currently working with one of my best friends at the time. As we walked away to our cars, I looked back and at the same time he was looking back at me. We both smiled an embarrassed smile and there was an instant connection. Jo Ann then informed me that he was a very nice man and a great youth pastor, but had just recently stepped down from ministry.

Over the next few days Rocky had started asking my friend that he worked with about me. Next, he called me. I wasn't sure exactly why he would want to call me. He said that he thought that I was really pretty and had heard good things about me. He then asked me for a dinner date. I told him that we could go as friends, but I assured him that I wasn't the one for him and that he really did not want to go out with me! He asked why and I explained about my past career and the fact that he was a former pastor. He did not judge me or act any different, but instead asked if I was saved, born again? Did I know Jesus? I said, "Yes" and he said, "That was all he needed to know". I said, "I had been saved about a year and a half. He said, "What time can I pick you up for dinner?" We became instant friends and started dating. There was a lot of chemistry between us; we dated off and on but I still had some unresolved issues with my past marriage that I needed to get through. Some time passed and I really felt that I wanted to pursue the relationship with Rocky, but I also knew that just as I had been hurt by the world along with personal decisions that I had chosen, Rocky had also been hurt by the church along with personal decisions that he had chosen. I felt like I was meant to be with him. I felt like he was my soul-mate. We were both wounded, but both knew the Healer! We both had a heart for ministry. I shared with him my vision about ministering to women. It seemed strange, at this time I was a fairly new Christian learning and increasing in my life. Rocky had been in the church since he was eleven, but had just stepped down from his youth pastor position. The hurt and disappointment had set in and he was experiencing decrease. Somehow I believe God's plan was for us to balance and complement each other. We did both have baggage; we both grew up fatherless, both understood poverty and unmet needs well, both experienced divorce and we both had two children. In June, 2000, we flew to the Bahamas, got married, and began a marriage and blended family. It has not been easy, but worthwhile. God is at the center of the marriage and He is the glue. Today, we've been married fourteen years! All glory to Him! We've learned a lot over the years and have been through many life experiences.

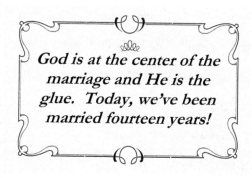

God is at the center of the marriage and He is the glue. Today, we've been married fourteen years!

During the majority of our marriage, we have remained attending Sheffield - now a mega church in Kansas City. My husband was on the Board of Directors at the church for many years. During all of these years I primarily sat in the congregation as a "bench warmer."

For a few years I was in the choir and went to events, of course, but was not living out my full potential. See I was a born again, saved Christian woman, set free from my past yet still held captive in the present. I was in bondage, fearful of being judged by the people "inside the church" wondering if they would ever find out about my past and if I could be transparent going forward. I was worried about how the people would feel about my past life. After all, I was a pastor's wife now and my husband was on the board! I played the part. I lived a Christian life, I was blessed and highly favored, I lived in plenty, we did not lack! We were tithers, we were faithful. There was no way I was going to make a move about ministry at this time because, in my mind, all I could think about was what would people say about my husband, kids or family? I had to protect them.

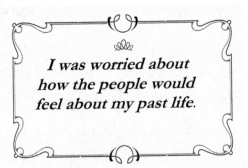

I was worried about how the people would feel about my past life.

By now I had seen and experienced hurt in the church as well...people are human. We are going to be human and battle a sinful nature in church as well as in the world! The only one who never sinned was Jesus! But at the time I was overly concerned because we did not know if Rocky would be restored to a pastoral position at this church and I did not want to bring him anymore shame. I was clearly in bondage; I was a prisoner unaware. I kept quiet, stayed to myself and trusted no one. This was not a good feeling and it went on for many frustrating years. During these church going years, I did keep thinking about going to another level and helping people.

I decided it may be beneficial for me to go to college. I think I enrolled for many reasons; I wanted to feel good about myself, accomplish something, and find out if I was capable of gaining a Bachelor's degree. I was looking for something to affirm my intelligence; something to say that I had more to offer than outward appearances. Something that said I was smart, capable and worthy. I enrolled in a community college, earning my Associate's degree in Arts and then I enrolled in Nursing College. In 2005, I graduated with my Bachelor's degree in Science of Nursing and passed the State Boards and became

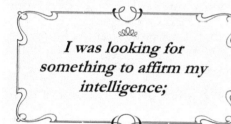

I was looking for something to affirm my intelligence;

a Registered Nurse. Still, I knew that I only wanted to work with women. I got a job as a postpartum mother-baby nurse and worked in the hospitals for a couple of years. I also worked at a psychiatric hospital, teaching outpatient day classes. I felt good about my achievement but not fulfilled. I still felt like something was missing. At this time, I was also struggling with fertility issues as my husband and I were trying to have a child together. In the meantime, my husband underwent a risky and expensive surgery. We knew our time was running out to have a child together. We looked into adoption, but something just did not feel right. I was diagnosed with thyroid disease and was feeling depressed. I was praying for answers to many questions.

Then one evening, Rocky was yelling upstairs for me to turn on the news. A girl was on the news and I did not want to miss this story!

I turned on the television and there was a girl on several national networks being interviewed about her pioneering a ministry into strip clubs! She was paving the way in California and Las Vegas! I was seeing my thoughts and vision playing out on national television! I was so excited that I went to the computer and wrote her a letter. This was in 2005. I am sure she was flooded with contacts! I never heard from Heather, but I was so glad to know that someone was actually

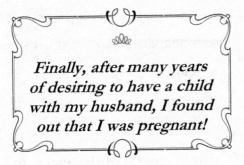

Finally, after many years of desiring to have a child with my husband, I found out that I was pregnant!

doing this! Finally, after many years of desiring to have a child with my husband, I found out that I was pregnant! I was so excited!! Until a few weeks into the pregnancy, I suffered a miscarriage. I was sad and devastated! Our new home that we had built sat with an empty nursery room for at least two or three years. I refused to give that room any other purpose. I was crying out and questioning God. I was living in a pure pity party; all kinds of emotions were flying. At the same time, God was doing some very emotional healing within my family. It was a turbulent time; I should have known that God had something awesome coming around the corner! I was experiencing loss and gain at the same time. I had been speaking to my father at this time as well as another sibling about some old, underlying family issues that needed to be resolved. I asked my father to do some DNA testing to reveal some answers and truth. The situation was volatile but necessary. It was a turbulent time in several homes of the family. But God is so good and His specialty is brokenness and restoration! All remains whole and well in our homes and with the information, lives made more complete.

My rightful birth information got corrected with my father's name on my birth certificate and my true last name was implemented. This was huge for me! It's very hard for a girl to grow up feeling father-less. I am so glad that I know now who I am - on earth and in heaven – a Daughter of the King! God, the most awesome Father! Even though emotions were high and battles were fought during this pe-riod, God still got the victory. I kept trying to conceive again but ulti-mately had to realize God must have another plan...

The Birth of Ministry

"Go into all the world and preach the gospel to every creature."
The Great Commission
~Mark 16:15 NKJV

"For I know the thoughts that I think toward you, says the Lord,
thoughts of peace and not of evil, to give you a future and a hope."
~Jeremiah 29:11 NKJV

"Redeemed" by *Big Daddy Weave*
Seems like all I could see was the struggle
Haunted by ghosts that lived in my past
Bound up in shackles of all my failures
Wondering how long is this gonna last
Then you look at this prisoner and say to me
"son stop fighting a fight it's already been won"

All my life I have been called unworthy
Named by the voice of my shame and regret
But when I hear you whisper, "Child lift up your head"
I remember, oh God, You're not done with me yet

Because I don't have to be the old man inside of me
'Cause his day is long dead and gone
Because I've got a new name, a new life, I am not the same
And a hope that will carry me home

I am redeemed, You set me free
So I'll shake off these heavy chains
Wipe away every stain, yeah, I am not who I used to be
Oh, God, I am not who I used to be
Jesus, I am not who I used to be
'Cause I am redeemed
Thank God, redeemed

"I would die 4 U" by *Prince*
I am not a woman, I am not a man
I am something that you'll never understand

I'll never beat you, I'll never lie
And if you're evil, I'll forgive you by and by

'Cause you, I would die for you
Darling if you want me to
You, I would die for you

You're just a sinner I am told, Be your fire when you're cold
Make you happy when you're sad, Make you good when you are bad

I am not human, I am a dove
I am your conscious, I am love
All I really need is to know that you believe

Chapter 4 Life-Giver
Seed Planter & Women's Missionary

I've often heard it said that God must have a sense of humor; I would have to agree! I believe He works in mysterious and wondrous ways! His ways confound the wisest! Although many years ago, great seeds of faith were released into my life, it was in 2010 that I truly conceived and became pregnant! I was pregnant with the calling and that same burning desire was stirred up and manifested in a desire to give. We had been tithers throughout our entire marriage but this was different. I recall lying in my bed one evening and reading a book by Mike Murdock about giving. I had never really given beyond our tithe. As I lay there I turned to my husband and said "You do know that our life is about to change?" It just came out of my mouth! Where did that come from I wondered? I had this deep feeling that I needed to sow a $1,000.00 seed into a ministry. This feeling lingered on for months…that year we went on vacation, one of our many trips to San Diego, California. We were so blessed by our boss to get to go on these "pleasure trips", paid in full for us! I've come to realize God had another plan for us and these trips. On this particular vacation, we happened to be in San Diego on a Sunday. My husband said "I know of this great church, the Pastor, Miles McPherson, came to Kansas City many years ago and preached for me at one of our youth camps." So we decided to visit. On our way out of the building, someone handed me a flyer regarding human sex trafficking. I found it to be interesting. As we returned to Kansas City, I began to do research on that church. To my surprise, there was an active women's ministry there that has a chapter of the Strip Club Ministry connected to Heather. I had written to her about the ministry that she pioneered. She was now ministering in Las Vegas. I was so excited! I immediately knew that this was where God wanted me to sow my $1,000.00 seed! I told my husband and the check for $1,000.00 went directly in the mail that day. Up until this time, I had never been one to talk to anyone I did not know and especially not on the computer. Since coming out of the sex industry after many years, I had been overly cautious of people and relationships. I knew I needed to come out of the protective shell to learn about the ministry.

I began speaking on the phone to one of the leaders and within a few weeks, in January of 2011, I flew to San Diego and joined one of their Bible studies. For the first time in eighteen years, I shared the truth about my story at a church during a Bible study! It was a very relieving, yet strange feeling! That night the leaders and I went out to minister in the community. We were in a busy, dirty area of San Diego and I was ready to go. I thought "I got this – no problem!" I thought I could do this with no problem; after all, I had lived this lifestyle for seven and a half years at one time. I was so wrong about my perception of how my experience was going to be! It was a small club, not many girls working and very, very dirty. As we were walking in, the doorman was super nice and friendly toward us but as soon as we got past the door, it hit me...smoke filled the room, the stage, and atmosphere. There was an overwhelming darkness that the Spirit now living inside me did not match. It was very intense for me walking back into that environment after eighteen years of being set free. I could see the girl on the stage and she appeared so lost. There was like a thick fog in this place. As we approached the dressing room, a group of other dancers were in another room on the left, perhaps avoiding the girls in the dressing room. We walked in and said, "Hi". We explained who we were and that we were from the church. There were only two very young girls in this dressing room and it

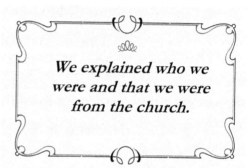

We explained who we were and that we were from the church.

was filthy; torn carpet, dirty, run down lockers, a small ledge and an old mirror. It was not fit for animals. It was very dirty and gloomy and my heart broke and sank for the girls. We treated them with kindness and left our cards with the church information on the make-up table. We left a beautiful fruit arrangement on the counter as well. One thing that shocked me and God revealed to me, was regarding the food we left for the girls. The ministry team must have really built a trusting relationship here because when I was in the industry, I would have never accepted food or drink from a stranger! When I was first delivered, years back, I suffered a lot of anxiety and struggled with food. A doctor had temporarily placed me on Xanax. God showed me that night, during the outreach, where the root of my problem with anxiety over food came from. That root is chopped down and no more food struggle exists, praise the Lord!

Next, as I remained in San Diego, we decided to go on another outreach. This was a night that I will remember for the rest of my life! Looking back, the one thing that prepared me was this: when I first originally flew to San Diego at the beginning of that week, I was reading "Reposition Yourself" by TD Jakes on the airplane. Then God showed me a scripture to hold on to in the Bible. I was nervous about going in the beginning, but the scripture He gave me was Proverbs 2: 7-8, "*He stores up success for the upright; He is a 'shield' for those who live with integrity so that He may guard the paths of justice and protect the way of His loyal followers*" (Holman CS Bible).

That night, as we went out to minister, there were three of us. I could immediately sense a very dark spirit in the club. There were things going on unlike any I had ever seen on the stage. The men were all seated along the wall and a very young man in particular appeared to be glaring as if he was in a hypnotic state; there was a haze-like appearance on his face, as he stared into the distance of the lights. My heart hurt for him; he appeared ill. Next, the leader headed back to drop something off in the dressing room and I stayed standing on the floor area when a girl came up to me. She said "Hi, I grew up a Christian!" I locked eyes with her immediately and felt the Holy Spirit prompt me to share my testimony quickly, in a nut shell. She said she had something she would like to share with me and wanted to talk so

180

we sat down. She began to explain to me that she was hooked on heroin and could not come to work without it, her boyfriend was the pusher. She said that her father had recently found out that she was a dancer because he walked into the club and saw her! She was getting upset talking about it and asked for prayer. I prayed for her to be delivered and set free from the drugs and to put a wall between her and the pusher and that when she was ready to make changes that the resources would be right there for her! She was so appreciative and took the card with the church information on it and said she was going to contact the church! My heart was overwhelmed! She got up and returned to the dressing room. The second she got up from me, a strange man, out of nowhere, swiftly sat down next to me. I thought "Oh great, this guy is going to try to flirt with me or talk to me…" It did not take long for me to recognize that this man was under demonic influence. I looked around for the leader and she was nowhere in sight.

He looked at me and asked, "Why are you here? What are you doing here? Are you here to take the girls out of here?" I said, "I am only here to tell the girls that Jesus loves them and we love them too."

He looked angry. He then asked me if I had ever fasted for forty days, I said no and he said "You better!" Normally in any situation like this I would be in a panic and anxiety ridden but the whole time he began coming against me verbally, I just sat there calmly and began, silently, calling on the name of Jesus, over and over. My eyes were combing the club, looking for the leader of the ministry. The man became angrier and told me that he did not like this at all and did not want me there. He was then sitting on the edge of his seat, angry. I sensed that he wanted to strangle me and hurt me, but he was <u>afraid</u> of me and he could not touch me. At the same time, I was still calling on the name of Jesus over and over in my mind, remained calm and next I sensed that there was an invisible shield around me, protecting me and I knew he could not touch me. My mind then reflected back to the scripture from Proverbs 2:7-8 that the Lord had given me on the airplane. I just remained still…inside HIS shield. Then the leader arrived, she sensed what was going on, came and stood directly in front of where we were sitting, pointed her finger at him and said "It's time to go!! We are about our Father's business!" His head dropped and he bowed his head to her then jumped up out of his chair and ran out of the strip club!! We were astonished and amazed at God's authority and power and protection! He ran out of that strip club as if it were on fire! He could not even stay in that den of inequity! God's Presence was in there!! After these experiences in California, I knew that this was a ministry with serious spiritual warfare and I needed to really get prepared before launching my ministry.

As I returned to Kansas City, a couple of weeks passed and God began to place on my heart to do it again! I questioned God, "Do what again? Another $1,000.00 seed?" I felt God say the answer was yes! Next, the ladies from California called me and connected me to Heather in Las Vegas; the girl, who I had written to in 2005, that had originally pioneered the ministry. We talked; I again immediately sent a $1,000 seed for the second time! I was so excited! Within a few weeks, in March of 2011, I was again, alone on an airplane, on a God-assignment to Las Vegas! I met Heather and her team of incredible women, went on an outreach and had a wonderful experience! I can say that I did again feel emotional after the club experience but my heart does melt every time. In Luke 10:30, Jesus Himself tells the story of the good Samaritan – when the Samaritan saw the <u>condition</u> of the man lying there, <u>half-dead</u>, he had <u>pity</u>, empathy, compassion and he helped the man up! Jesus told the religious scholar, "Go and do the same." I believe these are correct emotions to have but we must be careful not to judge or condemn or hold ourselves higher. I don't believe God elevated me and raised me to make it up to the top of the mountain to stay up there and never come down, help someone else or guide and direct them as to how to climb up the mountain! I learned much from both of my California and Las Vegas experiences. I learned different things from both ministries. My mind and heart were full of new knowledge, experience and questions about starting my own ministry in the Midwest. Surely this baby was crowning and I was entering the transition phase. I was in need of a "midwife" – someone to coach me on to the next level!

I returned to Kansas City once again and began to pray, prepare and talk with pastor's wives and pastors for advice and counsel. I was still <u>VERY</u> uneasy about sharing my story with everyone and had battled this over and over in my mind. The ministries I had the privilege to participate with had spoken with me about being an extension to them, forming another chapter. I wanted very much to do that but I felt in my spirit that I needed to explore my options and make sure of my direction. I was beginning to feel upset and restless about my connections and what I needed to do. What did God want me to do? Did He have another plan?

Just then a pastor that we knew, my husband's cousin, Pastor Murillo from SFLC had come by our house and we began talking about the ministry and my frustration and seeking direction. I knew something wasn't quite right. We prayed about it. Then he asked me if I knew of Lisa Bevere and I said, "No, I did not". He told me he felt like she would be a good resource and that I should listen to some of her messages, etc.

Later that night, I went to sleep and I had a very vivid and clear dream. *In the last days,' God says, 'I will pour out my Spirit upon all people. Your sons and daughters will prophesy. Your young men will see visions, and your old men will dream dreams. Acts 2:17 NLT.* The dream confirmed exactly a personal attack and what was "wrong" with my connection. My heart was pounding and my eyes opened, I sat up in the bed and woke my husband up and told him about the dream. God was speaking to me with clarity about my circumstances. Generally, if I had ever had a bad dream, I may feel anxious or get up in the night and get a drink or turn on the TV or something to help ease my thoughts and not feel so fearful. But this particular night, Rocky prayed and I was at total peace and began to drift back off to sleep. Just as my eyes had shut there was this bright, bold and illuminated vision of an animated film clip. It was a very specific and short film clip from the Disney film, "The Lion King". The clip was of Simba and his father, his father was looking down at him and speaking life into him for him to "remember who you are!" It was a very powerful message. I quickly dozed off to sleep. As I woke up the next morning, my feet hit the floor and I rubbed my head thinking "Why would I dream about the Lion King Movie clip?" I hadn't seen that movie in years; we do not have any small kids in the house – where did that come from? I felt like the message in the vision was directed toward my husband and me. I went to the kitchen to make a cup of coffee and turned on Christian television and there sat Lisa Bevere on the James Robison program, holding up her new book "Lioness Arising" – that did it! I thought, okay, the pastor was just asking me about Lisa Bevere, and what in the world is going on with all this lion stuff? She began to speak about her book and the issue of sex trafficking. My attention was caught, I was all ears! I knew God was speaking something to me. I got in my car and went straight to the bookstore and purchased "Lioness Arising". I am not a big reader; however, I read the book in three days! I was blown away by this prophetic word – just for me!

Within that three days, my prior dream regarding my ministry connection was perfectly revealed, played out just as in the dream and I knew God was directing me down another path! Next, I did something I had never done before – I went back to the Christian bookstore and bought the audio book to make sure I wasn't missing anything and put it in my car. I then looked up the video clip from the vision I had "Remember who you are!" and interestingly, the video clip matched the message I was reading and hearing in the book. I believe this was a prophetic message given through my vision that night. This is what appeared in the actual movie clip as I looked it up: Simba, the son, is looking down at his reflection in the water and cannot see the father, he only sees himself. He questions himself and appears with his head hung low. Rafiki tells him to look closer – that the father lives inside of him!! Then the father comes to him from above and speaks – Simba lifts his head. The father informs him that he has forgotten who he is so in turn he has forgotten his father. He tells him to look inside himself and acknowledge that he is "more" than what he has become and that he <u>must</u> take his rightful place in the kingdom (the circle of life)! Simba calls out to the father "How can I go back? I am not who I used to be! How can I turn this thing around?" The father calls out to him in truth: "You are my son (or daughter) – the one true king (or queen) you are my royalty, my heir. You must remember who you are!" I needed to remember who I was. Simba then runs after and toward the father saying "Please don't leave me!"

This is the perfect picture of what our Heavenly Father says to us! He desires a relationship with us and to use us for His Glory! 1 Chronicles 28:20 reads, *"Be strong and courageous. Don't be afraid or discouraged, for the Lord God, my God, is with you. He will not fail you or forsake you. He will see you through!"* As I sit in my office today, the very room that I saved to be my nursery, I look up above my desk at a picture. I have placed a picture of a bold lion with scripture inlaid beneath him *"Be strong and courageous. Do not be afraid; do not be discouraged, for the Lord your God will be with you wherever you go!"* Joshua 1:9 NLT. This powerful word of God, which came forth to me in a vision, combined with the prophetic message in "Lioness Arising", propelled me to rise up, walk and go forth to knock on the doors which were to be opened for this ministry. Next, I received a letter in the mail from a dear pastor who was in need of financial support for an important, upcoming mission's trip. God impressed on my heart to sow a seed of $8,500! Where was I going to come up with that!? I had never had thoughts like this before in my life nor dreams and visions. I had been blessed with two cars, so I felt that I should give one of my cars away. I took the personalized plates off of my silver convertible, drove to the pastor's house and signed over the title of my car to the church. I've never done anything like that in my entire life. I felt really good and was at peace about it. Next I was listening to Beth Moore's message regarding mission work and the words rang "Just go!" I knew I needed to "GO". I believed God was about to do some amazing things but I had no idea all that was in store...

Through the dream, vision, and the book, God gave me the name "The Lion's Beauty Queens" and the vision and purpose for the ministry. I called a girl at church that does web design and asked her to unload my brain on a temporary website. The website was created in around three hours! God gave me every detail. Now I needed a team of ladies to "go" knock on doors and make connections.

One obstacle still persisted; the greatest tool the enemy uses: FEAR! How could I really put myself out there like that; in front of everyone, our family, church friends, leaders and pastors? These were terrifying thoughts. I kept contacting pastor's wives and women in leadership whom I had trusted with this and already shared some. I just asked them to pray. I needed strength, wisdom, discernment, direction and to know that He was in the midst of every area for what I believed was planned for the ministry in Kansas City. I needed to get up off of the sofa! I felt like God was impressing on me to go start at one specific area in Kansas. Oh, to my dread – I thought, no this can't be!! I do not want to ever go back "there!" This was the same area in which I was carried out of almost twenty years ago! I went to counsel with a pastor about my feelings and try to gain some advice or plan on next steps. It was then that I knew I only had one person to count on and He was the Holy Spirit!

I continued to pray; it was now the summer of 2011. My mind was racing with thoughts of what to do. I decided to get up off of my comfortable sofa and go pick up the telephone. I called the club in which I felt specifically instructed and a man answered the call. I was nervous and just began sharing with him who I was and that I was interested in visiting the strip club and bringing gifts for the girls. He said he was the day manager and as we were speaking, I could hear him acting as the emcee and calling girls up on the stage through the microphone. Next, he explained to me that he knew who I was, actually that he had heard of a ministry like this because he was a former minister!! My heart sank and also leaped because now God had my full attention! No wonder this was where I was being instructed to go! He then told me to come and meet the night manager and gain permission. Wow!! Now I really needed to get prepared! I called the club across the street in the same area, the one I used to work in. The day manager was abrupt and said to call back at night. My stomach was turning and thoughts were spinning. Could I really do this? I drove to these places and prayed in the parking lots. It took a few more weeks to finally get the nerve up to walk back in these places, here at home, in Kansas City, which years past I was all too familiar with! I asked myself, who will go with me? What will be my plan? I needed a plan fast! I went to the computer and immediately ordered 100 pink Bibles.

In the meantime, I had met a girl through work, who sold us advertising. I had been working with her for over a year and <u>on my birthday in 2011</u>, she had taken me out for lunch. We were in a very nice restaurant on the Country Club Plaza and as we were talking, she began to share with me that she had this overwhelming feeling that she wanted to do some missions work and that she had gone on a missions trip when she was growing up. She expressed to me that she wanted to help people and that she loved giving presents! I smiled and light bulbs were coming on. Could this be who God was sending to join me on my upcoming journey? I told her that I wanted to share with her my testimony and the reason that I'd been traveling so much over the past few months to California and Las Vegas. We were both in tears and we could hardly eat lunch. She said "I am all in, I want to help you!" Elena's eyes flooded with tears and she said that I was the one who gave her a gift that day! Soon after that, I was at church and there was a girl who I knew over the past eighteen years but never really had talked to her. Every Sunday lately, it seemed that she was sitting close to us in service. She was pretty, had a heart for God and I knew she'd been hurt a lot and been through a lot of life experiences. We began talking and I asked her over to my home to share some information and a DVD. She was moved by the ministry and said she was ready to go with me! There you have it!! God put this team together...me, the story and visionary, Elena, the intellectual, proficient in excel, computer work and business (things I knew nothing about) and Starla, the heart, who was more tender and soft than I was! Now we needed to pray in finances and support but first, the hard part – could I really walk through the doors of my past?

Elena and I went for coffee that next week. As we were sitting at a Panera Bread Company, I looked at her and explained that I felt like I was ready to try this and felt like we just needed to go. She, the planner, pulled out her iPhone and said "Okay, let's go next Thursday, August 11, 2011!" My heart was pounding! Fearful and excited, I went home to prepare the pink Bibles and gift bags. As I prepared, I contacted several pastor's wives and women in leadership to pray be hind the scenes (which I still do today for every outreach) I knew I needed to take at least two other ladies to wait in the car in the parking lot for prayer and security as we were inside. I brought another girl who I knew was spiritually strong and would push me if I got weak. Angie and I walked in together for the first time. I was full of emotions. Shaking, my hands reached in my pocket and pulled out an old picture of myself from twenty years ago; made a connection with the night manager and he said yes, we could come back! We then traveled across the street to the club I used to work in. I had a sick feeling in my stomach; I was fearful, but in my other jeans pocket I had a scripture that I had written and a quote written by Joyce Meyer that talked about taking a risk and doing it anyway – "do it afraid!!³" I knew that Jesus had already walked before me and was with me. I knew that He knew what was behind the door, that just as I was once behind the door, so were many other girls who He loves as well – Daughters of the King!! After that, we drove to the downtown area and one of the girls mentioned a club that we were about to pass. She said "Let's just stop by there!" I said no way; this was a very bad area and way out of my comfort zone!! But then I started thinking about it and was aware that the Holy Spirit was working through her. I said "Okay, let's do it! Let's take a few gifts too!" There I stood, on the corner of a very scary street, full of darkness, a place I could have never imagined myself! I was shaking in my pink high heels as we walked in the club with only four gifts in our hands. As we passed through the door, I felt a peace rush over me. The management and bartender were very nice to us and there were exactly four girls working that day!

They were excited to receive a gift that had no strings attached – just love. We gained permission to return.

> **"Oceans (Where Feet May Fail)" by Hillsong United**
> *You call me out upon the waters*
> *The great unknown, where feet may fail*
> *And there I find You in the mystery*
> *In oceans deep, my faith will stand*
> *And I will call upon Your name*
> *And keep my eyes above the waves*
> *When oceans rise*
> *My soul will rest in Your embrace*
> *For I am Yours, and You are mine*
> *Your grace abounds in deepest waters*
> *Your sovereign hand will be my guide*
> *Where feet may fail and fear surrounds me*
> *You've never failed, and You won't start now*
> *Spirit lead me where my trust is without borders*
> *Let me walk upon the waters*
> *Wherever You would call me*
> *Take me deeper than my feet could ever wander*
> *And my faith will be made stronger*
> *In the presence of my Savior*

That day, on August 11, 2011, "The Lion's Beauty Queens" ministry was founded. We had two clubs say yes out of the four that we visited that day. We began organizing and planning and setting up the dates for a once a month packaging event and outreach following. On my birthday in 2012, The Lion's Beauty Queens were incorporated as a Missouri, non-profit organization (another confirmation of significance) and in September 2012, we gained 501C3 status; all under the direction and leading of the Holy Spirit! All glory and honor to Him! Today we are reaching out into 17 clubs monthly. With the expansion of our influence we are serving as missionaries outreaching in three states; Missouri, Kansas, and California.

On outreach one evening, we visited a club for the first time. The manager was a woman. I will never forget something that she said. The girls came back to meet with us and as we were handing out the gifts and passing out roses, she introduced us to the girls. She put her arm around me and said "Girls, this is Dana – she's one of us!" Obviously she relayed that message to set the girls at ease. When those words were spoken, my heart dropped to the floor. All those years of pretending; pretending to be some "perfect professional Christian", who had "arrived" and made it up the mountain...Now a pastor's wife, sitting in the congregation with my walls up. I wasn't really doing anything significant for anyone but for myself and my own family. Terrified that those around me would "see me", the real me! As I looked at those girls, hugs being exchanged between them and us, I thought to myself "On the outside, yes, I had changed, and on the inside, I had been born again, but the answer is truly 'YES', I am still one of you!" My blood still runs red, I am still not perfect, and I have not arrived. I still make mistakes and I am flawed. I still go through pain, difficulties and struggles, I am still a human being; one that deserves love, hope, value and dignity. One whose heart is priceless, a treasure and one whose name is lovely, "...*Who can find a virtuous and capable wife? She is more precious than rubies...*" Proverbs 31:10 NLT. I am the one who holds the title, Daughter of the King. It was one time during the ministry that I found myself, to feel relieved. I am finally okay with the girl I used to be. Although Brittany died many years ago, if I had never known her and her pain, then who would I be today? How would I have this type of compassion for lost and hurting women? Over the last eighteen years, I've been through a tempering process to fulfill His plan and purpose for my life – although it has not been an easy road, not a day or experience has been wasted. To the broken ~ "I am one of you!"

I cannot express the blessings that have been exchanged! We have planted thousands of seeds in a very short amount of time. Lives of dancers, managers, owners, bouncers and staff are being touched and, at times, customers! It is by far the most thrilling and fulfilling journey to walk with God. He makes all things NEW!! It is exciting to serve the Lord! He does things through us that are not humanly possibly! We take pink bibles, devotionals, worship music, gifts for the ladies and managers, baked goods, roses and flowers for each girl and at Christmas, gifts for the girls' children (as many of them are single mothers) and last but not least, pink Christmas trees for their dressing rooms. Each month a special letter is written to go into the gift bag; we are working as seed planters, building a bridge to fill the great divide, inviting and welcoming them to churches, Bible studies and sharing community resources. Our greatest hope is that one day, each heart that we touch will make a decision to accept Jesus, build an authentic relationship with Him, as Savior, and experience a rich, abundant and satisfying life in all that He has for them. For there is no greater decision a person can make than to say "YES!" to Jesus and accept Him as Lord and personal Savior!! Hillsong United has a song that says it best "When only love could make a way, could break these chains, You gave Your life in a "Beautiful Exchange"...

In closing, may I say to the church, the body of Christ – there are many seeds of greatness sitting in congregations today just waiting to be lifted and called forth. We can never judge a book by the cover or know who we are speaking to or what soil our words are falling on. We must be the hands and feet of Jesus and extend grace and mercy to people and love them right where they are. I am FOREVER thankful for the grace and acceptance that I received in January of 1994 at Sheffield Family Life Center in Kansas City, Missouri. Without that, where would I be today? In writing this, I've shared many details of my life's journey. It was never meant to glorify the details of the past or cause disrespect toward anyone. Much of it was FAR worse and darker than the sugar-coated suitcase of memories that I've opted to share. It is not my desire to shock the church and I am aware that there is no glory in details. However, I am standing here to say that God can use anyone – He's looking for availability!! If my story, which is His-story, can help ONE person and even if just ONE makes a decision for Christ, then it was worth it all! I am living proof, walking as a messenger and ambassador for Christ, and now I truly understand what it means to live "The Purpose Driven Life!"

All for Him, A Life Laid Down, A Surrendered Showgirl
Dana McCartney Candillo
Jeremiah 29:11

Epilogue
He Makes All Things 'New'

He makes all things "NEW!" (He who was seated on the throne said, "I am making everything new!" Then he said, "Write this down, for these words are trustworthy and true." Revelation 21:5 NIV)

Decades have passed and butterflies still hit my stomach and things start to spin each time my car crosses over into the city of Independence, Missouri. I rarely frequent those areas but when I do every street is filled with jaded and haunting memories. I can't help but flashback and relive pictures of the past. Each time I find myself jogging down memory lane of the 1970's, driving past the old house on Park Street, the only stable remnant of my childhood. In the spring of 1977, after the tragic death and funeral of my grandmother, my grandfather, Janis, and I stood in the front yard. My grandfather dug and dug with his shovel and we planted a beautiful white Dogwood tree in the memory of "mom". Years later, when the house was sold the new owner tore the tree down. It really bothered me that it was no longer there. For many years the house sat empty and vacant. It appeared weathered, run down, and rotting away, desolate and dead.

I still remember vividly, life as an innocent child and "Mom" daily walking me to the elementary school. I've often questioned what my life would've been like if she would've remained with me, here on earth. For a child, the death of a parent is unfathomable! For me, like an earthquake in a seven year old heart, it shook me to the core. Through my journey I've learned that all things work together for good for those who love Him. (Romans 8:28). In June of 2013 I was contacted by an old high school friend. She shared with me that she now worked for the city and that the city had recently purchased the condemned property. My old house was scheduled to be fully renovated for Habitat for Humanity to help "give back" to the community for a family in need. She had recognized my family surname on the title and thought to contact me regarding the restoration process. The house on Park Street was to be completely transformed and restored to its original historic state, in which it was in the early 1900's. Cheri had asked if I and/or my family would be interested in taking part in the city's ribbon cutting ceremony and dedication of the house upon completion. I said "Yes, of course!" After sharing with her she said she was making a special note to correct the missing dogwood tree in the front yard. She plans to have a "new" one planted. He makes all things "New"! When recently driving by, I've noticed the process has begun. All of the many outer layers of old vinyl siding have been peeled off and away. Underneath it all, original, handcrafted and beautiful scales of scalloped edged, chocolate colored, cottage style wood tiles perfectly aligned all along the house. I'd never seen or known they existed under the hard shelled siding. I am very excited and can hardly wait to see the finished, completed and beautiful

"New" Home. God's specialty is brokenness and restoration. He takes what is worn down, labeled condemned and dangerous and lifts it up- Restores and Renews and calls it "Lovely" and "True". He makes all things "New". Likewise when we look into the human heart and begin to strip away the entire hardened exterior, beneath all of the pain and scars from life, lays the protected original and unique state, tender, soft and pliable. When the true condition is exposed and vulnerable; it then is ready to be molded and shaped in truth by the Potter's hand. Once again it becomes fully ALIVE!

Rewinding and looking back to August 11th, 2011… once again I was driving down old roads and dark alleys of my former life…This time driving for hours until the day turned to night. We drove and drove across two states; Missouri and Kansas. We entered the gravel roads leading to parking lots of strip clubs on the outskirts of town, parking lots in the heart of the city and parking lots in the impoverished and run down urban core. In those parking lots we prayed and thanked God for this new found territory of opportunity. An opportunity to share His light and Love with other women. A place where some may say impossible to find "common ground". Walking back into the clubs here at "home" was one of the scariest things I've ever done! It was also one of the boldest and courageous. I have no more time for past regrets, that old life is far removed from me now; He makes all things "New".

That evening as I returned to my home, I walked into the kitchen and once again I was on my "comfortable" sofa. My husband and friends were all around me. They were really excited and kept talking about future things to come and how large the grand scheme of things could become. I began to get anxious, nervous and began to cry. My mind got worried and my heart overwhelmed with thoughts of attention being on me and people "knowing". I knew when we were outreaching to the women it was "right";. It was awesome. It was good. It was exactly what we were supposed to be doing. However, like Peter if we walk out on the water for a few minutes then take our intent focus off of Jesus we will begin to sink! When pain is our pulpit – It will drive passion, and passion like fuel will keep you going! It will keep you on the right path – The road to Glory!

"You have to know that your mission is so great, that you cannot afford to worry about what other people think. You must "GO" Anyway!"[2]

The Life of the Ministry

"God has chosen the foolish things of the world to put to shame the wise, and God has chosen the weak things of the world to put to shame the things which are mighty..."
~1 Corinthians 1:27 NKJV

"And when a great multitude had gathered, and they had come to Him from every city, He spoke by a parable: 'A sower went out to sow his seed. And as he sowed, some fell by the wayside; and it was trampled down, and the birds of the air devoured it. Some fell on rock; and as soon as it sprang up, it withered away because it lacked moisture. And some fell among thorns, and the thorns sprang up with it and choked it. But others fell on good ground, sprang up, and yielded a crop a hundredfold.' When He had said these things He cried, 'He who has ears to hear, let him hear!"
~Luke 8:4-8 NKJV

"Saints" by C3 Church Oxford Falls

The Joy in Me
I live and breathe
I Know it's from you
I know it's from you

You took my wrongs
Made them right
From darkness to light
Darkness to light

Let it fall
The hope you can give that's changing it all
Let it fall
The love you that's saving the world

Here we are, all the saints in rows
Singing Holy Holy
Here we are, all the saints in rows
Singing Glory Glory

The life that's real
That fire I feel
You're lighting it up
Lighting it up

No one else
Can save our souls
It's always been you
Always been you

In your light I'll follow

Chapter 5 Seeds
Ministry Information & Praise Reports

Lion's Beauty Queens:
1st outreach: August 11,2011

Praise Report:

On August 11th, 2011 The Lion's Beauty Queens set out to try to get into four adult entertainment clubs; two in Kansas City, MO and two in Kansas City, KS suburbs. LBQ members were able to deliver 23 gifts and 23 flowers to three clubs. However, one club that took the flowers asked us not to come again, and we were denied into one other club. LBQ members had beautiful packages containing pink bibles, The Father's Love Letters, candles, and beauty products. Three LBQ members entered the clubs, two members were praying in the car right behind. LBQ leaders were able to meet with the managers to gain trust. It was a successful night and we were invited back again for the following night!

Praise Report:

On September 22, The Lion's Beauty Queens had a total five members deliver over 50 gifts, 50 roses, and four managers' gifts to two nightclubs. Each present and rose contained a business card with church information it. Three of the LBQ members had created beautiful packages containing zebra printed journals with scriptures, Father's Love Letters and beauty products. A total of five LBQ members were on the outreach team and went on the outreach.

Praise Report:

Praise Jesus! One of the clubs that we were originally denied, opened their door to us! Fifty-seven gifts and 70 roses were delivered to girls in three nightclubs on October 20, 2011 Four members of the packaging team had created beautiful packages containing letters from LBQ, Hell Night Invites, flower printed journals with scriptures, candles, jewelry, and beauty products. Five members, took part in the outreach that night.

Lion's Beauty Queens @
SFLC WOMEN's Meeting: Feb 2, 2012

Praise Report:

Dana and the Lion's Beauty Queens were invited to Sheffield Family Life Center Women's Ministry meeting on Feb, 2 2012 to share testimonials and to introduce their mission.

Lion's Beauty Queens @ God's Chicks Conference
Los Angeles, CA
July 28th-30th 2012

God's Chicks Conference:

Part of The Lion's Beauty Queens mission is to learn and grow with this mission. On July 28th-29th, three of The Lion's Beauty Queens members and their security went to The God's Chicks Conference in Los Angeles, California. While there, LBQ members worshipped with well-known female ministers and leaders such as Holly Wagner with Oasis Church in L.A., Lisa Bevere, and Marion Jones. The God's Chicks Conference was all about freedom. Freedom from sex trafficking, freedom from addictions, freedom from anxiety, freedom. Only God can provide that true freedom to us! In addition, the LBQ members participated in the leadership breakfast to learn how to even become a more efficient leader. LBQ members left the conference spirited and ready to tackle even more tasks in The Lion's Beauty Queens ministry.

Praise Report:

Glory to God! Once again we met at Lee's Summit First Assembly of God for our HUGE Christmas packaging event. We were blessed to have over …. ladies helping us to package . Overall, we put together 120 ladies gifts, 105 kids gifts, 120 flowers, and 22 manager's gifts. The ladies gifts contained pink bibles and the Managers received "I am Second" book. Thank you to all who helped us out and donated their time and money. Not only did we bring in all of those presents, but most of the clubs also received a cute, decorated pink Christmas Tree and also pink cupcakes. Please see what Dana had to say about the 4 ½ hours long outreach to 7 clubs!

From Dana:

I stand amazed & in awe of God! His Love breaks down walls and bridges the great divide! Our Christmas Outreach was so exciting and full of Blessings! There were so many God moments…too many to count! I am going to list a few highlights:

*The girls had taken their own tip money and purchased gifts for us as well as items for our upcoming women's shelter donations.*A doorman said his brother is a Pastor and buys him books like this all the time, he thanked us.*Many managers, doormen, waitresses, bartenders received gifts and bibles.*One girl said she always wears her "cherished" bracelet. *I shared my testimony & gave a gift/bible to someone I knew 20 years ago…Only God.*Girls Loved their gifts. *One manager will only be there 6 more months...we will miss him.*A girl told us that she keeps a message bible that we had previously given her in her car and reads it all the time.*One manager said he has made copies of our list of resourc.es several times and girls have been taking them. One could never express or explain the actual ministry experience but to say "One extraordinary moment to the next." This is so thrilling, There is no High like the Most High…To Him, Be All Glory!

LION'S BEAUTY QUEENS
FEBRUARY 2013 OUTREACH

Praise Report:

The Lion's Beauty Queens met once again at Lee's Summit First Assembly of God to prepare our Valentine's Day outreach. The packages contained heart chocolate candy, beauty products, lotion and "Knowing God" cards. We also celebrated Dana's January birthday with cake and presents! Also, we launched our LBQ sweatshirts to help us out with fundraising (check out our photos). In addition to bringing our signature roses, packages, we also brought pink cupcakes to the ladies.

From Dana:

Last Night's outreach was an Extraordinary Event! Our Best outreach to date! To start off with a VERY unexpected donation to our ministry! FAVOR in all 7 clubs* A girl requesting a pink bible as she missed us last month! Girls were SO receptive at every club, New meetings with owners & managers. A girl writing down service times, says coming to church this Sunday! The MC in one club announced over the microphone "Lion's Beauty Queens are in the house", Thank them!!...Girls receiving gifts all throughout the clubs!! A VERY POWERFUL evening...difficult to write about as we must maintain confidentiality, but know JESUS is on the throne & moving. Amazing!

209

Praise Report:

As I prepare writing our Easter Outreach this is what keeps rolling around in my mind... "Because of the Lord's great love I have been redeemed." I thought about it a bit and isn't it true for each one of us? I wasn't redeemed because people judged me and told me what a horrible sinner I was. I wasn't redeemed because I go to church every Sunday. I'm not redeemed because I live a perfect, sinless life. There is one reason and one reason ONLY why any of us are redeemed, saved, delivered, set free and have had our slate wiped clean and that is Jesus and His great love for us. The Bible says in Heb 12:2 that "who for the joy set before Him, endured the cross, despising the shame." You and I are a part of His joy.

Only God allows us to be able to report back such incredible testimonies to our experiences in the clubs. We don't ever want to lose sight of that no matter how comfortable we may be in some clubs and the amount of favor and freedom we are given there, we know that it is ALL Him and for Him and unto Him that we serve that others may experience true, real love.

LION'S BEAUTY QUEENS
OCT EVENT: SFLC

Praise Report:

Reflection from Last Sunday @ SFLC: What an Awesome Sunday morning & the Peace that fell and rested in that place! I am confident that there was a shift, a shaking, and movement in the hearts of people This is His ministry and truly a representation of His Unstoppable Transcending Power! We are just Messengers....A small Praise Report of 3 things that really stood out to me after the services: 1) A woman came up to me with a donation in her hand, she expressed gratitude and shared that one of her family members is working in the industry and has encountered us and received gifts from us! 2) A man came to me tearful and thanked me for the work of this ministry, that he had been involved in the club life previously as well, as management staff. 3) A young 16 year old girl, pregnant...came to us for prayer and we were able to pray with her and direct her to resources of Mother's Refuge: A Christ centered home for teenage girls to receive care and comfort during and after pregnancy and a multitude of help!....Lastly, I am so thankful for the Peace that sustained me to share my story publically so that others may receive Hope in Him and Him Alone!.....

Praise Report:

Highlight: Equipping for Our Mission! @ Cherish "Brave" Conference 2013 in San Diego, California

"Spirit lead me where my trust is without borders, Let me walk upon the waters, Wherever You would call me, Take me deeper than my feet could ever wander and my faith will be made stronger in the presence of my Savior." Oceans by Hillsong United

Our trip to San Diego for the Brave Conference was incr...edible! As Dana stated on an earlier post it was a time of refreshing, equipping and building us up to prepare us and keep us fired up. I started this post with a quote from the song "Oceans" which was one of the worship songs at the conference. When I think of the ocean I think of words like magnificent, amazing, awesome, mighty, powerful, gorgeous, beautiful and yet also peaceful, calming and inspiring. That is like our God. He is all of these things and so much more!

Praise Report:

The love of Christ tears down walls, breaks chains, opens up the doors of the imprisoned and gives light when we feel we are in the darkest pit of our lives. We saw the results of the love of Jesus this month as we celebrated in thankfulness the love and favor of our God and how He has allowed us to represent Him as instruments of His love and power. "The Spirit of the Lord is upon me, because the Lord has anointed me to bring good news to the suffering and afflicted. He has sent me to comfort the brokenhearted, to announce liberty to captives, and to open the eyes of the blind." Isa 61:1

KS – Club #1 – We are welcomed in with open arms. One girl told us that we make the girls feel "special". The manager welcomes our return next month as we will be bringing gifts for ladies and their children! Club #2 – Continue to be welcomed to bring gifts and roses. Club #3 – Girls were immediately opening gifts. We were able to share and relate and let girls know they are loved! Club #4 – Dropped off gifts and roses for the girls and left extra gifts for the day girls. Very busy in there but girls still receptive to us. Club #5 – One girl expressed interest in her personal faith. Beautiful girls and all very thankful for the gifts, roses and love!

MO – Club #1 – Set up a complete turkey dinner for this special club. The girls were in awe and so very thankful. The manager told everyone to come back so that a blessing could be said over the meal. The girls kept hugging and thanking us and saying how much they loved us. They also wanted to know if we could stay and eat with them! Unfortunately, we had more stops and this was just the beginning of our night so we had to decline the offer. Although we were very touched by it. One girl is getting married and told us she wants us to come to her wedding. So sweet. Precious girls in this club. One girl says she has kept every rose we have ever given. Amazing! The doorman was also in awe of the gesture of bringing dinner in. Total disbelief but incredibly thankful! The girls' faces were absolutely glowing the entire time we were there. Love.In.Action. Awesome!

Praise Report:

Amazing Christmas Outreaches! 3 States~ Missouri, Kansas, & California! 7 Cities Covered! A Highlight/Praise report will be coming! 2 Things I cannot quit thinking about: 1) The sweet girl sitting on a sofa next to the stage & the pole with her opened gift and Pink Bible in her hands gazing down at it. 2) The Manager & Owner of one club gave us gifts that they said represented what we are to them! The gifts were beautiful angels! These last 2 nights have been tremendous Outreaches. I do know were making a difference...God is doing amazing things in these lady's hearts.....I just sit back in awe. We took 160 ladies gifts into the clubs; 34 Managers Gifts, Kids gifts and 9 White Christmas Trees! The scripture that keeps coming to me is Mark 16:15. Then he said, "Go into the world. Go everywhere and announce the Message of God'...s good news to one and all. (the message) .Wednesday night December 11, 2013 1st Club...Door Man & Bartender were very receptive. The manager was excited to receive a gift! The girls were very thankful for the Children's gifts. 2nd Club Doorman no longer there. 3rd Club Manager was very welcoming & invited us to come back anytime, so appreciative. 1 girl applying for other jobs. She was very engaged with us.

4th Club Collected gifts for donations to Women's Shelters....

5th Club The manager Lights Up when we come in. One of the girls already opened her gift and was holding & looking at her Pink Bible, sitting next to the stage.

Praise Report:

Last Night was a night that I would call a night of connections...It's obvious that strong trust and relationships have been built. I stand Amazed each time at the way in which we are welcomed. Some managers literally come out to the parking lot or come out to the street when we pull up to greet us, hug us, and usher us in! They are excited for us coming and know that we are there to bring "good" for their girls! It literally lights up the night! This happened 3 times last night as we went to 5 Clubs! Some of them call us their "church ladies"... But what's so cool is that they do not fear us & I feel they love us "back". In the past people have put rude condemning & judging flyers on cars in parking lots, said and done ridiculous things trying to convert people!! Christians: That behavior Does Not work! It's awful & damaging! The only way is LOVE & GRACE!--The reason HE came to this Earth!.....Love Creates Transformation: It Worked For Me!!

Praise Report:

Kansas City/Warrensburg Outreach~ As we entered into the 3rd club of the night we were immediately announced over the mic by the DJ/Manager: "Lion's Beauty Queens are in the House"~"Cuz we all love us some Jesus"!!! Wow, What a welcome! Lots of faces we've known over the last few years are now gone....Lots of reports of new jobs, education decisions, and moving forward. One "house mom" met us in the parking lot and talked for quite some time. Plans are in the works for another upcoming support group! One great surprise, one of the managers at a particular club is a lady who has never spoken much to us, shown in ways that she didn't really care for us coming in and has never been very friendly toward us to say the least....last night a complete turnaround! She LOVED the big beautiful pink roses, her face lit up, had eye contact and conversation with us and thanked us!! She seemed very appreciative and like a different person. A changed heart! Lives being Touched, Lives being Healed, Hearts being Transformed. Dana

Testimonies

Twenty years ago I was a lost young lady looking for love and affirmation in the darkest of places. I was enticed to dance in the world of Gentleman clubs local and nationwide, blinded by what I thought was a glamorous acceptance and spotlight. After years of trying to fill a void within myself by working in the industry, my spirit became weary. At my lowest point I found Jesus. I married a pastor's son, submerged my life in church, began my new saved life and started a family. I knew I was saved and forgiven but was I really healed? I thought I was…until 20 years later when God has a plan to completely free me from a world of hurt I had only tucked away in shame. Not only was he going to heal me, but he would free me by using me as a voice in an industry I never thought I would revisit. I had never heard of the Lion's Beauty Queens nor had I heard of any ministry coming close to touching this specific industry. I could not believe they could get in the door! LBQ has found favor in these clubs by showing the most pure and raw love of Jesus, a love with no strings attached and no conditions. The dancers are like bugs to the light; they can't resist the love, the hugs, the gifts, and he warmth. This love is like no other!

I am so honored to now be a part of the LBQ team and to shine a different light, His light, a beacon for the lost.

Anna

We have, for years, been blessed by the service and consideration of "The Lions Beauty Queens." Aside from the joy shown by our ladies at the gifts they bring these ladies make themselves available for all types of ministry, from inviting the employees to church sponsored events, to availing themselves when someone is hurting or struggling. I have even heard a girl say (on two different occasions), "This is the first Bible I have ever owned" (upon receiving one of the many Bibles they have handed out). One other girl asked for a second gift package to get a Bible for her son. If we believe "the Word never comes back empty" then that is reason enough for their ministry. In this time of strife, judging and placards it is refreshing to find women with Christian ideals just coming in and loving these employees. Having read the Bible I never saw Christ carry a placard or help pass legislation. He just loved, taught and helped the hurting. Everyone needs love and many of our girls are hurting. The "Lions beauty queens" offer both. They exemplify Christ and reflect His ministry in a place that few others do. In taking into account the ministry of these ladies please reflect on the words following some of Christ's most famous words. John 3:17 "For God did not send His Son into the world to condemn the world, (some versions say "judge") but that the world might be saved through Him."

Sincerely,

Bob, Club Manager

The Lions Beauty Queens are great. We all look forward to the ladies coming to see us and remind us of how much they love us and care for us. They are always grateful for seeing us. They are truly a gift from God. I hope they can keep doing what they are doing. They truly make a difference. I have been a club manager for 20+ years and I feel so blessed to have met these ladies.

Thank You,

Mary, Club Manager

Hello, my name is Rene,

I have been a dancer on and off for the last 12 years in a couple different states. I have to say that I have never seen a group like the Lions Beauty Queens. When the Queens come into the club I can always count on them listening to my stories without passing judgments. They always come bearing gifts and flowers. What girl doesn't like presents and flowers? Flowers always have a way to make you feel good no matter what is happening and that is what these flowers do. Brighten up your day! Not to mention they are being gifted to you by a woman that has probably walked in your shoes.

The gift packs that I have received in the past have always had literature included, that seem to know where most of my pain was based….. Losing my father at age 15 always has had a huge effect in my life and I am sure I don't speak for myself when I say "I have daddy issues." I can say that I feel like these ladies relate to dancers and that is what put them aside from the church down any street. The respect they carry for themselves and others shine! I have always felt grateful when they visit and I know some of the girls, feel the same way. To know there are people and places we can be respected and not judged means a lot!

I would like to thank the Queens for always bringing light into what can be a dark place! I still have my Bible that was given to me Christmas 2012 and I plan on keeping it for life. Thank you Lions Beauty Queens.

Love,
Rene, Dancer

Words cannot express how grateful and thankful I am to have such compassionate, beautiful sisters come and show us such loving support. You always seem to arrive just when we need you most and always leave us with a spiritual uplift and positive outlook.

God has blessed us to the fullest with such beautiful angels to remind us that we are loved and remembered always as God's children. God bless you all and remember that words cannot ever express how much love we have for you guys.

Love,

Emma, Dancer

Thank you for everything that you do. It has made an impact on my life for the better. I do hope we get to continue to enjoy the ladies who come in on behalf of our souls.

Megan, Dancer

"Break Every Chain" by Jesus Culture
There is power in the name of Jesus
To break every chain

All sufficient sacrifice
So freely given
Such a price
Bought our redemption
Heaven's gates swing wide

There's an army rising up
To break every chain

"I Give Myself Away" by William McDowell
Here I am , Here I stand
Lord, my life is in your hands
Lord, I am longing to see
Your desires revealed in me
I give myself away

Take my heart
Take my life
As a living sacrifice
All my dreams all my plans
Lord I place them in your hands

I give myself away, I give myself away
So You can use me
I give myself away, I give myself away
So You can use me

My life is not my own
To you I belong
I give myself, I give myself to you

Sex Trafficking

Statistics and Information

- ℘ Human trafficking generates **$9.5 billion** yearly in the United States. *(United Nations)*

- ℘ Approximately **300,000** children are at risk of being prostituted in the United States. *(U.S. Department of Justice)*

- ℘ The average age of entry into prostitution for a child victim in the United States is **13-14** years old. *(U.S. Department of Justice)*

- ℘ A pimp can make **$150,000-$200,000** per child each year and the average pimp has 4 to 6 girls. *(U.S. Justice Department, National Center for Missing and Exploited Children)*

- ℘ The average victim may be forced to have sex up to 20-48 times a day. *(Polaris Project)*

- ℘ Fewer than 100 beds are available in the United States for underage victims. *(Health and Human Services)*

- ℘ Department Of Justice has identified the top twenty human trafficking jurisdictions in the country:" Houston • El Paso • Los Angeles • Atlanta • Chicago • Charlotte • Miami • Las Vegas • New York • Long Island • New Orleans • Washington, D.C. • Philadelphia • Phoenix • Richmond • San Diego• San Francisco • **St Louis** • Seattle • Tampa *(Department of Justice)*

- ℘ A pimp can make **$150,000-$200,000** per child each year and the average pimp has 4 to 6 girls. *(U.S. Justice Department, National Center for Missing and Exploited Children)*

- ℘ **One in three teens** *on the street will be lured toward prostitution within* **48 hours** *of leaving home. (National Runaway Hotline)*

According to U.S. Federal law, human trafficking is defined as:

- Sex trafficking in which a commercial sex act is induced by force, fraud, or coercion, or in which the person induced to perform such an act has not attained 18 years of age; or
- The recruitment, harboring, transportation provision, or obtaining of a person for labor or services, through the use of force, fraud, or coercion for the purpose of subjection to involuntary servitude, peonage, debt bondage, or slavery.

According to the United Nations, human trafficking is defined as: Recruitment, transportation, transfer, harboring or receipt of persons, by means of the threat or use of force or other forms of coercion, of abduction, of fraud, of deception, of the abuse of power or of a position of vulnerability or of the giving or receiving of payments or benefits to achieve the consent of a person having control over another person, for the purpose of exploitation

Modern Day Slavery:

Human trafficking is also known as modern day slavery. Human trafficking deviates from our historic view of slavery, making it hard to conceptualize. But ultimately, slavery today and 200 years ago share the same notion: It's the notion that one person's life, liberty and fortune can be under the absolute control of another, and be sold, bought, or used at the will of the owner.

U.S. Statistics:

Human trafficking exists all over the United States, but California is California is a hot spot for domestic and international human trafficking because of its large population, international borders, large economy, extensive ports, and metropolitan regions.

- The average entry age of American minors into the sex trade is 12-14 years old. [1]
- Many victims are runaway girls who have already suffered sexual abuse as children.

- California harbors 3 of FBI's 13 highest child sex trafficking areas in the nation: Los Angeles, San Francisco, and San Diego. [2]
- Foreign nationals are also brought into the U.S. as slaves for labor or commercial sex through force or fraud. [3]

The prevalence and anonymity of the internet has fueled the rapid growth of sex trafficking, making the trade of women and children easier than ever before.

About the Author

Dana McCartney Candillo, BSN, RN

As a child Dana endured the death of a parent, father in prison, dysfunctional environment of alcoholism, drug addiction, poverty, abuse, neglect and was sexually abused by the age of 8. She went onto a troubled adolescence, promiscuity, and using alcohol and drugs herself to cope with pain. Despite dreams of college and a career in modeling, that pursuit ended in beauty contests, bikini contests and finally trafficked into exotic dancing through a local tanning salon. Dancing in strip clubs all across the Midwest became "the life" for 7 ½ long years. Her first marriage to a male stripper/drug dealer ended with him at the gates of a prison. Now a single mother, sheer survival became her personal hell. Dana had experienced God as a young child and had an authentic experience with Him as a teenager. She felt His hand of protection was on her all the time dodging risks and avoiding calamity. As the illusion of "the Glamorous life" derailed and was de-escalating to a rapid halt...She felt the words, "Love has taken over me- I have been set FREE". In January of 1994 she encountered a Divine Appointment and a Divine Rescue as she surrendered it ALL to Jesus at the altar at Sheffield Family Life Center in Kansas City, Mo.

She went on to marry a youth Pastor in the church in 2000. They have been married for 14 years with 4 children and 4 grandchildren. She went back to college, earned her Bachelor of Science Degree in Nursing and is a Registered Nurse. Though God had spoken to her many years prior about a women's ministry which required returning to the strip clubs, it wasn't until several years later she felt released to this calling. Dana founded The Lion's Beauty Queens, a Kansas City based ministry reaching out to women in the sex industry on August 11th, 2011. On her birthday in 2012 the ministry was incorporated and gained 501c3 status. Her ministry was birthed through a dream and vision that God gave Dana and her inspired reading of "Lioness Arising", a book written by Lisa Bevere. Walking in a new strength and boldness Dana returned to the strip clubs, this time bringing gifts, flowers, resources, ministry invitations and LOVE with no strings attached.

The LBQ ministry has grown into several teams and another chapter ministry outreaching to a total of 17 strip clubs throughout Kansas City, Missouri, Kansas and California. Our mission is to empower and encourage women letting them know they are loved, valued, and purposed.... a Daughter of the King. Dana is extremely passionate about seeing women set free and discovering a real and authentic relationship with Jesus Christ, a personal decision in their own timing. She also believes in the Church being a safe and healing place where people are met right where they are and extending grace, time, and power to change and experience truth, revelation and restoration. One life transformed... one life at a time.

Enjoyed this one. Stay tuned for Dana's forthcoming book
Before Brittany

For more information or to support The Lion's Beauty Queen's ministry, please write to us at:

Lion's Beauty Queens, Inc.
P.O. Box 6425
Lees Summit MO, 64064
Email: lionsbeautyqueens@yahoo.com
Website: www.lionsbeautyqueens.org

DR GEORGE W. WESTLAKE, JR
PASTOR EMERITUS
SHEFFIELD FAMILY LIFE CENTER
5700 Winner Road, Kansas City, Mo 64127
816-241-LIFE

February 5, 2014

TO WHOM IT MAY CONCERN:

I am happy to recommend the ministry of Dana Candillo "THE LIONS BEAUTY QUEENS," a wonderful, God anointed outreach.

This is a great ministry, which God placed into the heart of Dana, and is very effective in reaching those ladies who are involved, or have been involved, in the sex industry.

Not only is this ministry unique, it is a ministry of great compassion and it is extremely effective in demonstrating the Love of God to those who may feel they are outside the area of His love.

I have known Dana 20 years and her husband Richard (Rocky) for 40 years. They are a dedicated, consistent, loving Christian couple with a desire to reach as "many people in as many ways possible."

The undersigned has pastored in the inner city of Kansas City for over 40 years and people of our congregation have been in involved in a lot of ministries. THE LIONS BEAUTY QUEENS is one of the greatest ministries for reaching people that no one else is reaching.

Let me encourage you watch the video, let this ministry touch your heart, and if possible, add your support to reach these ladies for The Lord Jesus Christ.

in JESUS CHRIST,

George W. Westlake, Jr., DMin

"If you cling to your life, you will lose it; but if you give up your life for me, you will find it."

~Matthew 10:39 NLT

References

Biblical References

Bible Gateway by Zondervan © 2012
Holy Bible: New Living Translation by Tyndale © 2006
Holy Bible: King James Version by Zondervan © 2000
New American Standard Version by Foundation Publication Inc. © 2002
Holman Christian Standard Bible by Holsman Publishing © 2010

Quotes

1. T D. Jakes, The Potter's House – Dallas, Texas
2. T D. Jakes, The Potter's House – Dallas, Texas
3. Joyce Meyer, Joyce Meyer Ministries—Fenton, Missouri

Songs

The Story of Beauty by Destiny's Child *Album: Survivor © 2011*
Not Afraid by Eminem *Album: Recovery © 2010*
Wash Away Those Years by Creed *Album: Human Clay © 1999*
Dead Flowers by Miranda Lambert *Album: Revolution © 2009*
Welcome to the Jungle by Guns & Roses *Album: Appetite for Destruction © 1987*
Simply Irresistible by Robert Palmer *Album: Heavy Nova © 1988*
Time After Time by Cindy Lauper *Album: She's So Unusual © 1983*
I Would Die for You by Prince *Album: Purple Rain © 1984*
Redeemed by Big Daddy Weave *Album: Love Come to Life © 2012*
Oceans Where My Feet May Fail by Hillsong *Album: United © 2013*
The House that Built Me by Miranda Lambert *Album Revolution © 2010*
Break Every Chain by Jesus Culture *Album: Awakening Live From Chicago © 2011*
I Give Myself Away by William McDowell *Album: As We Worship Live © 2009*
Saints by C3 Oxford Falls *Album: Saints © 2014*

Statistical Data

http://caseact.org/learn/humantrafficking/
CASE ACT 2011. All rights reserved.